© Stonewell Healing Press, 2025
 All rights reserved.

This book is a labor of care. Please do not copy, share, or distribute any part of it—digitally or physically—without written permission from the author or publisher, except for brief excerpts used in reviews or critical articles. Your respect helps this work reach others who need it.

This workbook is not a replacement for therapy, crisis support, or mental health treatment. It's meant to offer reflection, comfort, and growth—not clinical care. If you're struggling, please reach out to a licensed professional. You matter too much to go through it alone.

Every effort has been made to ensure this content is accurate, responsible, and thoughtful. The author and publisher cannot guarantee outcomes and are not liable for misuse or misinterpretation of the material.

Thank you for being here. We're honored to walk beside you.

M. Tourangeau
Stonewell Healing Press

TABLE OF CONTENTS

SECTION 1 -   1
When Love Turns Heavy

SECTION 2-   33
Where the Story Fractured

SECTION 3 -   63
Naming What's Unspoken

SECTION 4 -   93
Setting Boundaries Without Guilt

SECTION 5-   127
When You've Grown Apart – And You Miss Each Other

SECTION 6   161
When You Feel Like You're Always the One Trying

Stonewell Healing Press

TABLE OF CONTENTS

SECTION 7 -   193

Resentment or Realism – When It Feels Like You're Always Giving More

---

SECTION 8-   255

When Letting Go Means Finding Peace, Not Giving Up

SECTION 9 -   283

The Echoes Around You – How Outside Forces Shape Your Resentment

---

SECTION 10 -   333

Building Your Peace – Practical Steps to Move Forward

SECTION 11 -   363

Who You Choose to Be Next

CLOSING   392

Stonewell Healing Press

Dedicated to those who are stuck in survival mode.

STONEWELL HEALING PRESS

HOW TO USE THIS WORKBOOK

Take your time with this. The more you pause to really think about each question and answer honestly, the more space you create for reflection. And with deeper reflection, this experience can open up new understanding and healing you might not expect.

Be honest with yourself—there's no judgment here. This is your private space. If you want, you can even throw this book away or burn it later to keep your secrets safe. That said, be mindful of how much you dive in. Healing and reflection around tough, sensitive topics can bring up strong feelings—and yes, it can get triggering. So here's your gentle trigger warning.

The real progress comes when you practice the skills, not just read about them. The more you try them out in your life, the more helpful this workbook will be.

STONEWELL HEALING PRESS

ASSESSMENT

WHERE AM I NOW?

Before we begin, take a moment to honestly check in with yourself by rating these statements on a scale from 1 (not at all) to 10 (completely):

1-10

1 I can recognize when my nervous system is being triggered before it controls my reactions.

2 I feel able to respond to conflict with intention rather than being pulled into automatic reactivity.

3 I can distinguish between genuine connection and the illusion of intensity or chaos in my relationships.

4 I feel confident expressing my needs and maintaining boundaries without fear or guilt.

5 I am able to protect my emotional energy and sense of self, even when others are volatile.

6 I notice recurring patterns in my emotional responses and feel equipped to shift them consciously.

7 I can stay grounded, clear, and centered even in moments that used to overwhelm or destabilize me.

8 I trust myself to reclaim peace, resilience, and autonomy, regardless of what others do or say.

SECTION ONE

When Love Turns Heavy

There's a moment — sometimes quiet, sometimes explosive — when something shifts. You still care. You still want it to work. But something between you feels heavier now. You snap more. You withdraw more. You hold on to things longer than you used to. The connection that once felt soft now feels... loaded.

Resentment creeps in like that. It's rarely one big betrayal. It's the unspoken expectations, the conversations that never got closure, the way you feel alone even when they're sitting right beside you. And the worst part? You still want the relationship. You're not trying to walk away. You're trying to find your way back — but it's hard to rebuild trust when you're the one carrying all the unprocessed weight. This workbook isn't about blaming you or fixing you. It's about helping you make sense of what you're holding, what you've swallowed, and what you actually need to feel peace again — whether or not your partner changes.

Making Sense Of It
The Hidden Architecture of Resentment

Sometimes resentment shows up as silence. Not the peaceful kind, but the kind where words press against your chest and never make it out. You swallow them down, over and over, until they sit like stones in your body. Each unmet need, each brushed-off comment, each time you felt alone while still in the room with someone you love — those stones collect. What begins as discomfort hardens into weight, and soon you're carrying more than the relationship itself.

The human nervous system doesn't easily forget unfinished business. Neuroscience shows that unresolved conflict lingers as what psychologists call "open loops." The body keeps reacting as though the problem is still happening, because in many ways, it is. You replay the argument while driving, hear their dismissive tone as you try to sleep, feel your jaw tighten during dinner. Even if nothing is said out loud, your body is reliving the imbalance on a loop. That's why resentment often feels exhausting — it's not just emotional, it's neurological.

In sociology, one of the oldest truths about human relationships is reciprocity. Across cultures, bonds are built on mutual exchange — of care, labor, attention, even small gestures. When that balance breaks, it doesn't just create frustration; it triggers a survival alarm. Your system reads it as "something about this bond isn't safe anymore." That's why resentment can feel so destabilizing. It's not simply that your partner forgot the dishes or didn't ask about your day — it's that your need to matter, to be considered, to exist as an equal presence in the bond, was quietly denied.

Making Sense Of It
The Hidden Architecture of Resentment

Anthropologists studying families have noted how much of this imbalance is invisible. Often it isn't the dramatic betrayals that leave the deepest marks, but the subtle, repeated ways love is unevenly distributed. One person keeps track of birthdays. One person smooths over tension after fights. One person notices moods and adjusts. Over time, that emotional labor creates a tilt so steep it's impossible not to feel it in your bones. Resentment is the protest of the one left holding that tilt alone.

It can be tempting to frame resentment as "anger you shouldn't feel." But if you look closely, underneath it is longing. If you truly didn't care, there'd be nothing left to resent. The very presence of resentment is proof that part of you is still invested — that you still hope to be seen, heard, and met in the way your heart aches for. That's what makes it so confusing: love and disappointment living side by side, each pulling you in opposite directions.

Resentment also works like sediment in water. A single grain doesn't change much. But when years of small hurts, dismissals, and unmet needs settle without resolution, the riverbed of your relationship shifts. The water can't move the same way. Even joy or intimacy becomes filtered through the layer of what's unspoken. And unless it's stirred up and acknowledged, that sediment quietly reshapes the whole current.

Making Sense Of It
The Hidden Architecture of Resentment

If you've carried resentment, it doesn't mean you're bitter or incapable of forgiveness. It means your emotional system has been doing its job: keeping track of imbalance, warning you that your well-being matters, pushing you to seek repair or change. Resentment is not the enemy. It is information — raw, sometimes painful, but always instructive.

The path forward isn't to deny it or explode under its weight. It's to listen. Resentment tells you where your needs have gone unanswered, where your boundaries need strengthening, and where your voice deserves to be heard. If you can meet it with curiosity rather than shame, resentment can shift from being a silent burden to being the compass that points you back toward yourself.

Where does resentment show up in your relationship?

Think about specific moments or patterns. What happens, and how does it feel in your body?

Where does resentment show up in your relationship?

What needs have gone unspoken in this relationship?

Instead of judging yourself, try to notice what you've needed but haven't felt safe to say.

What needs have gone unspoken in this relationship?

When did you start feeling like you had to shrink, over-function, or keep the peace?

Explore the origin of the silence. Was it one moment? Or slow and cumulative?

When did you start feeling like you had to shrink, over-function, or keep the peace?

What part of you feels unacknowledged or invisible here?

Is it the part that tries the hardest? That forgives first? That always notices what needs doing?

What part of you feels unacknowledged or invisible here?

What are you scared will happen if you ask for more?

Sometimes we don't speak up because we're not just afraid of being denied — we're afraid of being resented in return.

What are you scared will happen if you ask for more?

Do you feel like you're the only one who notices the tension?

Explore how that experience has shaped your emotional presence in the relationship.

Do you feel like you're the only one who notices the tension?

Have you ever felt punished for being hurt?

This isn't about blame — it's about truth. Has your pain ever been met with defensiveness instead of care?

Have you ever felt punished for being hurt?

What would you say if you could be 100% honest and safe?

Write the conversation you wish you could have, even if it never gets spoken out loud.

What would you say if you could be 100% honest and safe?

TRACING THE TRUTH

THE WEIGHT IN THE BACKPACK

Resentment often feels like carrying a backpack you never agreed to wear. Every unspoken frustration adds another stone. The first ones don't feel too heavy, but after a while, you can barely move.

Why it helps:
This gives resentment shape and form, instead of letting it stay as a vague fog. When you can see which weights are crushing you most, you can start deciding which ones are yours to keep carrying — and which you're allowed to release.

Close your eyes and imagine your resentment as a backpack filled with stones.
Name each stone after a recurring hurt (e.g., "the times I felt dismissed," "the unshared household work").
On paper, list these stones in order of weight — which feels heaviest, which feels lighter.
Circle one stone you're ready to set down, even if just for a while.

TRACING THE TRUTH

THE WEIGHT IN THE BACKPACK

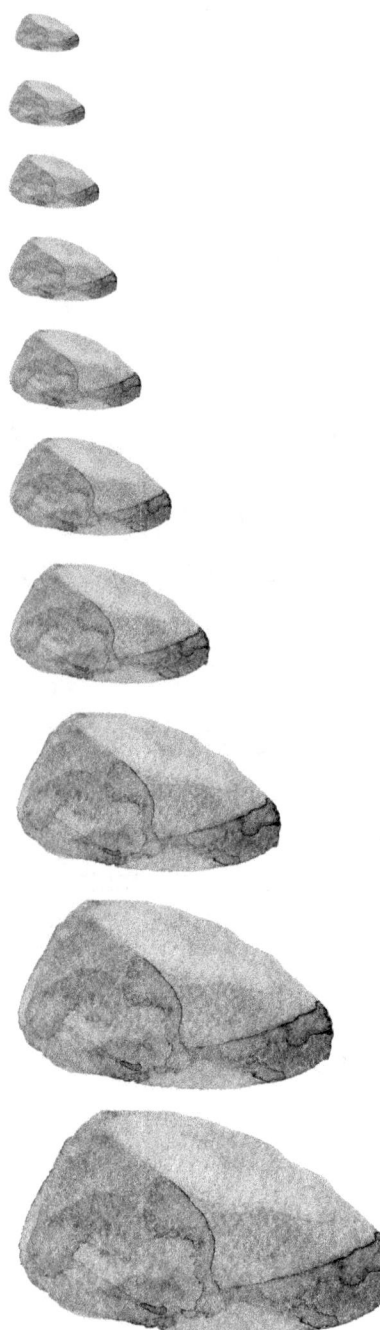

TRACING THE TRUTH

THE CLOSED DOOR, THE OPEN WINDOW

Resentment closes doors — to trust, intimacy, and communication. But even when a door is stuck, sometimes there's still a window. This exercise helps you notice the small openings.

Why it helps:
Resentment often thrives when we believe there's no way through. Finding "windows" reminds you that communication doesn't have to be all or nothing — even small openings shift the air inside a relationship.

Write down one situation where resentment keeps the "door" shut (e.g., "I can't bring up money without feeling angry").

Now, ask yourself: Is there any window here? Could the conversation happen in a smaller, softer way? Could it be framed differently?

Write one "window sentence" — a way to express the need without forcing the door open. *Example: "I know money is stressful, but I need to feel like we're a team in it."*

TRACING THE TRUTH

THE CLOSED DOOR, THE OPEN WINDOW

Situation

Potential Window

Window Sentence

TRACING THE TRUTH

CLEARING THE SEDIMENT

Imagine a glass of water with dirt stirred in. If it sits untouched, the dirt settles to the bottom, layering the whole cup. That's what resentment does when left unspoken.

Why it helps:
Resentment builds from unspoken layers. By sorting through the "sediment," you can see which hurts need clearing, which are still floating near the surface, and which may not belong in your glass at all anymore.

Look at the glass on the next page. Inside the glass, write down small recurring hurts that have "settled" (e.g., "they never ask how I'm doing," "I'm always the one planning").
Next to each hurt, note whether it feels like surface-level sediment or something deep and layered.
Pick one and write: If I stir this up and speak it aloud, what outcome am I afraid of? What outcome would I hope for?

TRACING THE TRUTH

CLEARING THE SEDIMENT

TRACING THE TRUTH

CLEARING THE SEDIMENT

REFLECTION

EXTERNALIZE THE INNER CRITIC

The inner critic often masquerades as truth, when really it's a protective part gone overboard. By externalizing it — drawing it, collaging it, or writing it as a character — you create distance. Suddenly, it's not you failing; it's a scared or rigid part doing its job too harshly. Research in IFS and narrative therapy shows that putting dialogue on paper softens shame and restores self-leadership. Adding a Wise Friend voice gives you access to compassion and balance. The final boundary statement reminds the critic: its role is protection, not punishment. That's where healing starts.

Create the Critic — Draw, doodle, or collage how your inner critic might look. Don't worry about artistic skill.

Dialogue — Write a short back-and-forth:
You: "I hear you saying I'll fail."
Critic: "I don't want you to get hurt."
Wise Friend: "You can protect without tearing down."

Set a Boundary — End the dialogue with a firm line: "Your job is protection, not punishment. I'll take it from here."

MAPPING YOUR RESILIENCE

When life is painful, the spotlight lands on what's broken or lost. But every hard season you've lived through also carries evidence of your resilience. Mapping your past with a "strength lens" helps you reclaim those forgotten skills — endurance, creativity, boundary-setting, persistence, humor, or compassion. Trauma research shows that naming and revisiting these strengths rebuilds self-trust. Instead of seeing your past only as a string of wounds, you begin to recognize the ways you showed up for yourself. Circling three core strengths creates a personal toolkit you can consciously bring forward into your next chapter.

1 Draw Your Timeline —Mark a few "hard seasons" you've lived through on the timeline.

2 Name Strengths — Under each event, write one or two strengths you used to get through (e.g., courage, asking for help, persistence).

3 Circle Three — Look at the whole map. Circle three strengths that feel most alive, relevant, or needed for where you're headed now.

4 Carry Them Forward — Write them on a sticky note or card where you'll see them often — reminders that you've done hard things before, and you will again.

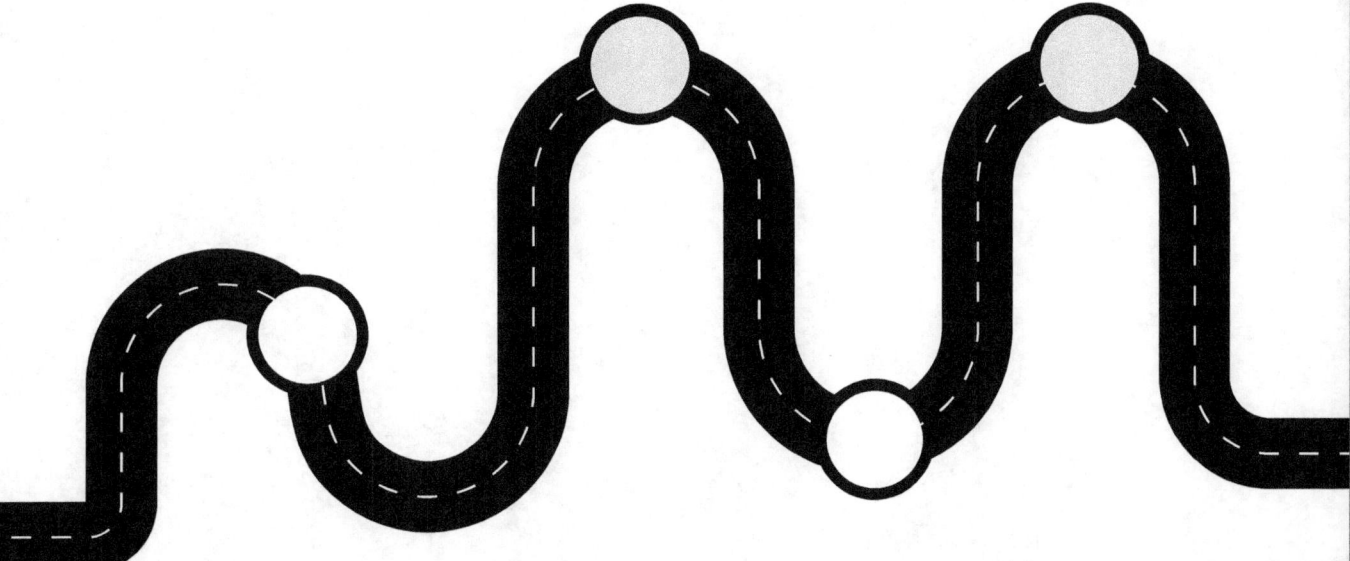

SECTION TWO

Where the Story Fractured

Every relationship has its turning points — the moments when the story shifts from hopeful to heavy, even if you don't notice right away. Sometimes it's a single conversation that went sideways, other times it's a slow accumulation of disappointments, misunderstandings, or unmet needs that never found their way out.

This section is about tracing back to those fractures — not to assign blame, but to understand how patterns started. When did small silences become walls? When did kindness begin to feel like a transaction? When did you start wondering if the "us" you believed in was more a wish than reality?

Knowing where and how things cracked open isn't about reopening wounds. It's about shining a light on the cracks so you can start rebuilding — with or without your partner's awareness. Healing begins when the story gets told honestly, and your experience finally gets the respect it deserves.

Making Sense Of It
Understanding the Fractures That Shape One-Sided Relationships

Some cracks appear gradually, almost imperceptibly, until one day the surface feels too fragile to bear weight. In one-sided relationships, these fractures don't happen overnight. They form from repeated micro-insults to your emotional system: the small dismissals, the missed promises, the moments your feelings were minimized. Your nervous system keeps score long before your mind catches on, recording tension, fatigue, and that creeping sense of invisibility as the subtle architecture of imbalance.

Your brain is wired to make sense of inconsistency, to protect you from unpredictability in relationships. When your efforts aren't mirrored, the mind searches for explanations: "I must be too sensitive. I'm asking too much. Maybe I'm the problem." This isn't self-criticism for the sake of shame — it's the adaptive survival mechanism your psyche developed to try to restore control where control was never really possible. These thought patterns, repeated over months or years, become a lens through which every interaction is filtered, making small slights feel catastrophic and leaving your internal scale perpetually off-balance.

The social frameworks around us often deepen the fracture. Many cultures glorify self-sacrifice and emotional labor as markers of commitment, especially in close relationships. When those societal messages collide with a relationship where effort is consistently one-sided, you internalize a skewed definition of worth: that your value is measured by how much you give rather than how much care you receive. The fracture isn't only relational; it's systemic, intertwined with norms and expectations that have shaped your perception of love and fairness.

Making Sense Of It
Understanding the Fractures That Shape One-Sided Relationships

Physical sensations tell their own story. A tightening in the chest, a hollow ache in the stomach, the fatigue that lingers after emotional investment — these are not random reactions. They are your body recording imbalance, a somatic echo of repeated disappointment. Recognizing these signals is crucial: the fractures exist both in events and in the neural pathways that formed in response. Your body remembers, even when your mind has learned to rationalize or normalize the inequity.

Humans thrive on emotional reciprocity. From an anthropological perspective, co-regulation — the mutual soothing, responding, and attuning to one another — is essential for relational health. When co-regulation fails, especially repeatedly, trust erodes. You may find yourself questioning your own perception: Was I too demanding? Am I overreacting? The fractures distort internal calibration, making it harder to know what healthy connection looks like, or even what you truly need.

Tracing the moments of fracture is an act of radical clarity. It's not about cataloging blame, but about mapping patterns: the conversations that left you feeling unseen, the small gestures that were never reciprocated, the silence where affirmation should have been. Each fracture is data — a piece of evidence that explains why emotional exhaustion, resentment, or doubt have taken root. Recognizing them allows your nervous system to release the tension it has carried silently, giving your mind context and your heart permission to feel without guilt.

Making Sense Of It
Understanding the Fractures That Shape One-Sided Relationships

Understanding where and how the story fractured also reframes your role. The fractures do not indicate failure; they indicate endurance. They show how consistently you sought connection in a system that could not sustain it. These insights empower you to distinguish between what was yours to manage and what was never under your control, and they provide a framework for how to show up differently for yourself moving forward.

By shining light on the fractures, you reclaim the narrative. The story shifts from "What did I do wrong?" to "What can I see now?" The cracks become instruments of insight rather than sources of shame. They teach you what signals to honor, which needs to advocate for, and when to step back from imbalance. The fractures are not marks of defeat; they are signposts for healing, guiding you toward clearer boundaries, self-compassion, and the ability to cultivate connections that are mutual and sustaining.

When did you first notice the relationship start to shift?

Pinpoint a moment or period when things began to feel different — what did you feel and notice inside?

When did you first notice the relationship start to shift?

What small, everyday moments felt like cracks in your connection?

Sometimes it's the forgotten birthday or the tone that wasn't soft. What added up for you?

What small, everyday moments felt like cracks in your connection?

How did you react when these cracks appeared?

Did you speak up, stay silent, or try to smooth things over? How did those choices affect you?

How did you react when these cracks appeared?

What emotions have stayed with you from these moments?

Name them honestly — anger, sadness, confusion, or loneliness. Each feeling has meaning.

What emotions have stayed with you from these moments?

What have you learned about yourself through this experience?

Have you discovered strength, patience, or ways you protect yourself?

What have you learned about yourself through this experience?

How have these patterns affected your connection with your partner?

Has distance grown? Has communication changed? Notice the impact without blame.

How have these patterns affected your connection with your partner?

Where do you see hope — either for the relationship or for yourself?

Even a small glimmer matters. What possibilities feel real to you?

Where do you see hope — either for the relationship or for yourself?

What would it feel like to tell this part of your story without shame?

Imagine speaking your truth fully, knowing you're heard and respected.

What would it feel like to tell this part of your story without shame?

TRACING THE TRUTH

TELLING THE STORY OF THE FRACTURES

Sometimes the story only makes sense when it's on paper. This exercise helps you track the key moments where the relationship shifted, without judgment or blame.

Why it helps:
By visually mapping the fractures, you can see patterns you may have internalized. It externalizes the story, reducing the power of self-blame and creating clarity about what was within your control — and what wasn't.

Look at the three columns on the next page: Event, Your Reaction, Emotional Impact.
List events or turning points in the relationship that stand out — small slights, repeated patterns, or major disappointments.
In the middle column, write how you reacted emotionally and physically at the time.
In the third column, note the ongoing emotional effect these moments had on your trust, self-worth, or energy.

TRACING THE TRUTH

TELLING THE STORY OF THE FRACTURES

Sometimes the story only makes sense when it's on paper. This exercise helps you track the key moments where the relationship shifted, without judgment or blame.

Event	Your Reaction	Emotional Impact

TRACING THE TRUTH

TELLING THE STORY OF THE FRACTURES

Sometimes the story only makes sense when it's on paper. This exercise helps you track the key moments where the relationship shifted, without judgment or blame.

Event	Your Reaction	Emotional Impact

TRACING THE TRUTH

MOSAIC OF EXPERIENCE

Relationships are made up of countless small moments, both positive and negative. Creating a "mosaic" allows you to hold the full picture without oversimplifying or idealizing it.

Why it helps:
The mosaic approach shows how individual fractures combine to shape the relationship dynamic. Seeing it visually reinforces that no single moment defines the whole story, helping you gain perspective and validate your lived experience.

On a blank sheet, draw a grid.
Fill each square with a memory, emotion, or moment that contributed to the current state of the relationship — include both good and difficult experiences.
Color-code or symbol-code each square (e.g., red for hurt, blue for love, gray for confusion).
Step back and observe the mosaic as a whole: patterns, clusters, gaps, and repetitions.

TRACING THE TRUTH

MOSAIC OF EXPERIENCE

TINY WINS PROTOCOL

When you're overwhelmed, your brain can trick you into believing nothing is possible. Big goals feel impossible, so you stall. But tiny actions build proof: I can move. Completing a single small task sparks dopamine — the brain's reward chemical — and that fuels momentum. Instead of waiting for motivation, you create it by acting first. Two-minute wins keep you out of the freeze state and remind you that forward movement doesn't need to be dramatic to matter. Over time, stacking these little completions can shift your entire day — and even your sense of self. It's not about doing everything; it's about proving to yourself that you can do something.

Pick a micro-task: Something that takes under 2 minutes (wash mug, text back, stretch, shower).

02 Countdown launch: Mental health awareness helps reduce stigma, promotes empathy, and encourages open conversations about mental health concerns.

03 Complete & log: Write it down or check it off for a small hit of satisfaction.

04 Notice momentum: Let the success energy carry you into the next doable action.

05 Repeat daily: Build trust with yourself through small, steady proof points.

THREE PILLARS BEFORE NOON

When you're caught in anxiety, depression, or burnout, your nervous system can swing between shutdown and overdrive. The quickest way to steady yourself is to touch three key areas: body, mind, and pleasure. Moving your body brings energy online; completing a mastery task (even something small like an email) restores a sense of competence; and engaging in pleasure reminds you that joy and safety are still accessible. This "trio" isn't about being productive — it's about balance. Think of it as a daily reset button. By noon, if you've already touched your body, completed one mastery task, and tasted one moment of pleasure, you've laid down anchors for resilience. Instead of asking your day to be perfect, you give yourself three touchpoints that prove: I can show up, I can accomplish, and I can enjoy.

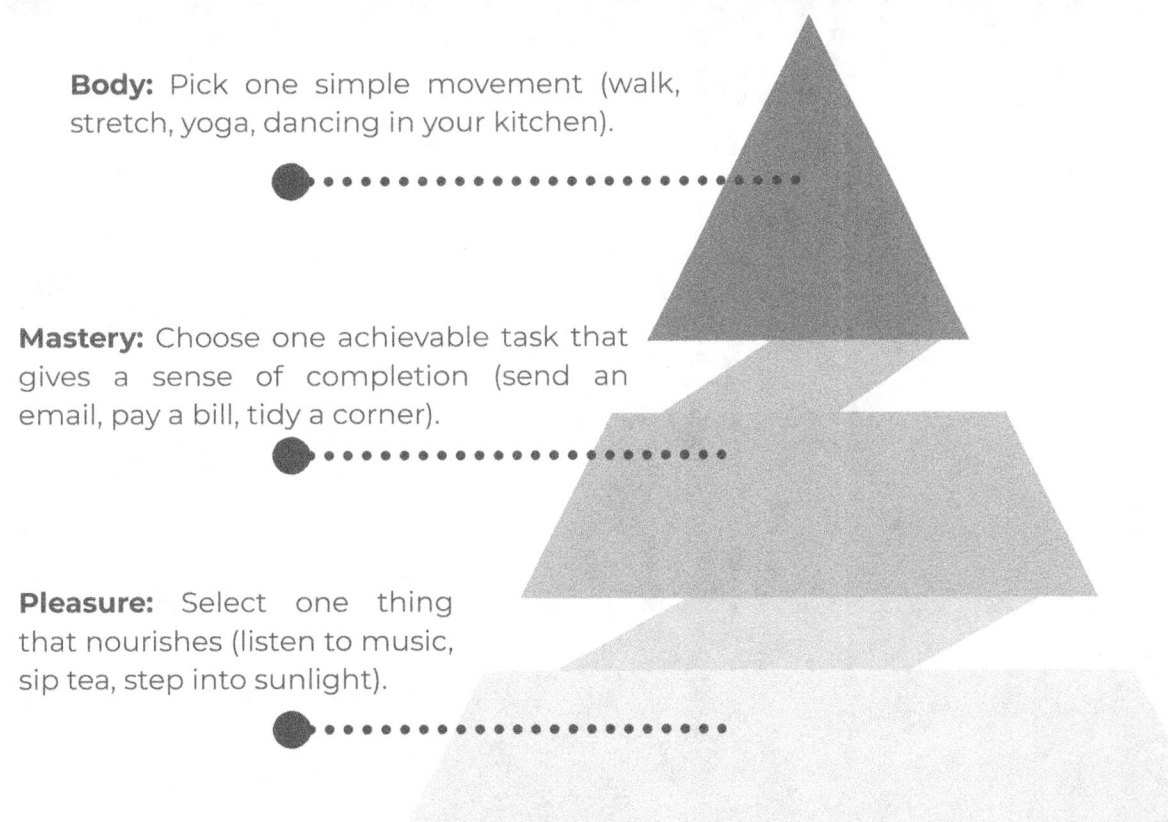

Body: Pick one simple movement (walk, stretch, yoga, dancing in your kitchen).

Mastery: Choose one achievable task that gives a sense of completion (send an email, pay a bill, tidy a corner).

Pleasure: Select one thing that nourishes (listen to music, sip tea, step into sunlight).

Stack them early: Aim to complete all three before noon to set your rhythm.

Reflect briefly: Notice how touching all three domains shifts your mood and energy.

SECTION THREE

Naming What's Unspoken

The heaviest parts of resentment are often the things left unsaid — the unmet needs, the hopes you buried, the boundaries you never voiced. Silence can feel safer, especially when you fear rocking the boat or triggering another fight. But what stays unspoken doesn't disappear. Instead, it collects weight, shaping how you show up in the relationship — guarded, tired, or simply distant.

This section is about giving yourself permission to name what you've kept inside. Naming doesn't mean dumping blame or airing grievances to hurt. It means being honest with yourself about what matters to you and what you need to feel seen and respected. When you learn to hold that truth gently — without shame or fear — you reclaim your voice and build a foundation for clearer communication.

Even if your partner isn't ready or able to meet you there, this is about your healing and choice. When you get clear about what you want and need, you start steering your relationship — and your life — toward something better.

Making Sense Of It
The Weight of Silence

Silence carries more than absence—it carries meaning, emotion, and often, unseen burden. In one-sided relationships, the things we don't say accumulate like sediment in a riverbed. Each unspoken desire, unvoiced boundary, or buried disappointment layers upon the last, subtly shifting the current of our emotional life. Over time, these silent weights manifest in tension, withdrawal, irritability, or the quiet erosion of self-trust. Psychology tells us that unexpressed needs don't vanish; they are internalized, often translating into somatic tension, chronic stress, or patterns of people-pleasing designed to keep the peace at the expense of the self.

Neuroscience reveals that the brain processes unspoken emotional experiences similarly to trauma. The amygdala, which governs threat response, reacts not just to immediate danger but to internalized emotional conflict. When your needs are consistently ignored, or when you silence yourself to avoid conflict, your nervous system registers that suppression as ongoing threat. Over time, this leads to hyper-vigilance, emotional fatigue, and sometimes, dissociation—a subtle "checking out" from parts of your own life. You're not failing; your body and brain are responding to prolonged relational imbalance as best they know how.

From a social and anthropological lens, the pressure to remain silent is not random. Many cultures, family structures, and relational patterns reward compliance and silence, particularly in environments where care is conditional or emotionally inconsistent.

Making Sense Of It
The Weight of Silence

Children raised in such dynamics often learn early that speaking up risks punishment, rejection, or withdrawal of affection. As adults, this translates into hesitation to voice needs, compounded by shame or fear that asserting yourself is "selfish" or destabilizing. One-sided relationships, by their very nature, exploit these learned patterns—intentionally or not—because the imbalance thrives when one person's needs remain invisible.

Emotionally intelligent approaches show us that naming what is unspoken is not confrontation—it is reclamation. Giving language to your desires, boundaries, and frustrations allows you to see them clearly and hold them with integrity. It transforms diffuse tension into discernible, manageable elements, creating a roadmap for self-awareness and action. Journaling, self-dialogue, or even speaking your truth into an empty room activates the prefrontal cortex, strengthening executive control and fostering a sense of agency. In other words, articulating what you've kept inside literally changes the way your brain processes relational stress.

Finally, consider the relational dimension: when you can identify your unspoken needs, you are no longer unknowingly projecting frustration or resentment onto interactions. The burden shifts from covert accumulation to conscious clarity. You may not immediately receive acknowledgment or change from the other person—and that's okay. The act of naming is a boundary in itself: it declares, "This is what matters to me. I am visible to myself." That is where empowerment begins. Even in the absence of reciprocation, clarity anchors your decisions, your emotional energy, and your sense of self-worth.

Making Sense Of It
The Weight of Silence

Silence is heavy. Naming lightens it. Not because your partner or the other person suddenly understands or changes, but because you reclaim authority over your own emotional life. Each word you articulate to yourself—whether spoken, written, or felt in a mindful reflection—is a claim on your truth. The unspoken no longer drifts silently; it takes shape, guiding your choices, your boundaries, and the way you care for yourself. Over time, this practice rewires not just your relationships, but the most important one: the one you have with yourself.

What have I avoided saying because I was afraid of the response?

Fear shapes silence. Naming it breaks its hold.

What have I avoided saying because I was afraid of the response?

What needs or feelings have I hidden to keep the peace?

Peace that costs your voice isn't peace at all.

What needs or feelings have I hidden to keep the peace?

How do I feel physically when I think about speaking up?

Body awareness can guide you to what's ready to be released.

How do I feel physically when I think about speaking up?

What would it look like to say one honest thing this week — even if it's small?

Start small. Every step counts.

What would it look like to say one honest thing this week — even if it's small?

What fears come up when I imagine being truly heard?

Fear often means you're close to a breakthrough.

What fears come up when I imagine being truly heard?

How have I silenced myself in this relationship?

Awareness is the first step toward change.

How have I silenced myself in this relationship?

What parts of me want to be heard the most?

Listening inward helps you speak outward.

What parts of me want to be heard the most?

What is my intention for my next honest conversation?

Setting an intention gives your voice power and purpose.

What is my intention for my next honest conversation?

TRACING THE TRUTH

NARRATIVE LETTER TO THE "SILENT YOU"

Sometimes the part of you that stays silent needs acknowledgment and compassion. This exercise connects you to that internal voice.

Why it helps:
Sometimes the part of you that stays silent needs acknowledgment and compassion. This exercise connects you to that internal voice.

Write a letter addressed to the version of yourself that remained quiet in the relationship.
Describe what that version experienced, what it needed, and what it deserved.
Offer understanding, validation, and support, as if you were a caring friend.
Close the letter with a statement of your intention to honor those needs moving forward.

TRACING THE TRUTH

NARRATIVE LETTER TO THE "SILENT YOU"

TRACING THE TRUTH

NARRATIVE LETTER TO THE "SILENT YOU"

TRACING THE TRUTH

NARRATIVE LETTER TO THE "SILENT YOU"

TRACING THE TRUTH

NARRATIVE LETTER TO THE "SILENT YOU"

PREPPING FOR TRIGGERS

Triggers often feel like they ambush you out of nowhere. But the truth is, many of them are predictable. By anticipating where you might get pulled off-center, you remove the element of surprise — and that's half the battle. A trigger plan sets you up with choice: which skills you'll lean on, what words you'll use, and how you'll protect yourself if things get too intense. Instead of being at the mercy of the moment, you walk in knowing you have backup. The post-event debrief closes the loop, helping your nervous system learn that you can encounter stress and recover, without slipping into shame. This practice builds confidence, resilience, and the quiet reminder that you're not powerless — you're prepared.

01. Predict

Think about the upcoming event. What likely triggers might show up? Write them down.

Pick two calming or grounding strategies you know work for you (breathing, stepping outside, orienting).

02. Choose skills

03. Script yourself

Prepare one short phrase you can use if you need to step back (e.g., "I need a minute, I'll be right back.").

Decide where you can go if you need space — outside, bathroom, car, or even leaving entirely.

04. Exit plan

05. Debrief with kindness

Afterward, check in with yourself. What worked? What was hard? Offer compassion, not critique.

SHELF IT FOR LATER

Sometimes intrusive images or thoughts crash in like uninvited guests — too loud, too vivid, too much. Trying to "not think about it" only makes them louder. Containment gives your mind a safe boundary. Instead of battling the thoughts, you acknowledge them, then choose to store them somewhere secure until you're resourced enough to revisit them (ideally with therapeutic support). This isn't avoidance — it's wise pacing. By practicing containment, you send a message to your nervous system that you're in charge of when and how you engage. It builds trust with yourself, lowers overwhelm, and allows you to get through the present moment without drowning in unfinished business.

Visualize a container
Pick something sturdy — a jar, vault, chest, box, or even a digital safe.

Name the intrusion
Briefly identify the image, memory, or thought you want to contain. Write it in this jar here.

Place it inside
Imagine physically setting it in the container.

Seal it shut
Hear the latch click, see the lock turn, or feel the heaviness of the lid close.

Store it away
Place the container on a high shelf, deep cave, or secure room in your mind.

Return only with support
Remind yourself you can revisit it later with a therapist, journal, or trusted guide.

SECTION FOUR

Setting Boundaries Without Guilt

Setting boundaries in a relationship often feels like walking a tightrope — balancing your needs with your love and fear of pushing your partner away. When resentment builds, it's usually because something important has been crossed or ignored, and you haven't felt safe enough to say no.

This section is about learning how to set clear, healthy boundaries without guilt or apology. Boundaries aren't walls meant to shut others out; they're bridges to respect and understanding. They help you protect your emotional well-being and communicate your limits in a way that fosters connection rather than conflict.

You'll learn how to recognize where your boundaries have blurred or disappeared, why that happened, and how to reclaim your voice with compassion for yourself and your partner. Setting boundaries isn't just about keeping resentment out — it's about inviting love to show up in ways that feel safe and true.

Making Sense Of It
Boundaries as Emotional Architecture

Boundaries are less about putting people out and more about defining the structural integrity of your inner world. Imagine your emotional life as a building: without clearly marked walls, floors, and support beams, everything starts to sag. Over time, small cracks appear—tensions in your body, frustration that rises and spills, exhaustion that accumulates. These cracks are often invisible until a small stressor collapses a part of the structure. In one-sided relationships, these cracks can grow unnoticed because your energy has been spent reinforcing areas that don't hold mutual weight.

The human brain is wired for connection, and social neurobiology explains why saying "no" triggers discomfort. We are designed to anticipate social rejection, to avoid conflict, and to protect bonds—even at personal cost. In one-sided relationships, this wiring becomes a trap: the part of your brain that seeks safety overrides the part that knows your needs are valid. Emotional labor increases, and cortisol—the stress hormone—accumulates. Over time, this neurobiological pattern can leave you exhausted, irritable, or emotionally numb, even when your conscious mind knows the relationship is imbalanced.

Psychologists and sociologists note that early attachment patterns heavily influence how we tolerate boundary violations. If you grew up in environments where saying "no" led to shame, punishment, or emotional withdrawal, your adult self may struggle to assert limits without guilt. You might override your own needs to maintain perceived harmony, unconsciously sacrificing self-respect for connection.

Making Sense Of It
Boundaries as Emotional Architecture

This creates fertile ground for resentment: a slow, simmering buildup of unmet needs that can eventually feel like a tidal wave of anger or despair.

The anthropology of human groups shows that cultures have long relied on implicit rules and unspoken hierarchies to maintain cohesion. Yet, when those hierarchies prioritize one individual over others—or allow consistent disregard for mutuality—the system becomes unsustainable. Similarly, your emotional ecosystem can't function without equilibrium. Healthy boundaries are a form of self-advocacy, a method of communicating your internal rules clearly so that others can respect them—or reveal their inability to do so. Boundaries are data, not punishment: they show what can be carried, what must be adjusted, and where mutuality fails.

Practicing boundaries without guilt requires cultivating two capacities simultaneously: self-knowledge and empathy. Self-knowledge allows you to detect what drains you and what energizes you. Empathy allows you to hold space for another's feelings without sacrificing your own. You are not responsible for managing another person's discomfort. Guilt arises when we conflate care for others with the need to protect ourselves—but guilt is a socialized emotional reflex, not a moral imperative. Recognizing this distinction transforms boundaries from "rejection" into an act of emotional architecture: a deliberate, sustainable design that preserves your energy, reduces resentment, and models integrity in relationships.

Where in my relationship do I feel my boundaries have been crossed?

Notice moments when you felt uncomfortable or ignored.

Where in my relationship do I feel my boundaries have been crossed?

What boundaries have I been hesitant to express, and why?

Fear of conflict, loss, or judgment can keep you silent.

What boundaries have I been hesitant to express, and why?

How do I feel physically and emotionally when my boundaries are respected?

Tuning into this helps clarify what you truly need.

How do I feel physically and emotionally when my boundaries are respected?

What messages did I receive growing up about setting boundaries?

Your family history can influence how comfortable you feel with limits.

What messages did I receive growing up about setting boundaries?

How does resentment connect to blurred or missing boundaries in my relationship?

Identifying this link is a key step toward change.

How does resentment connect to blurred or missing boundaries in my relationship?

What small boundary can I practice setting this week?

Start with something manageable and observe how it feels.

What small boundary can I practice setting this week?

How do I respond when my boundaries are tested?

Recognizing your patterns helps you respond intentionally.

How do I respond when my boundaries are tested?

What support or resources do I need to strengthen my boundary-setting?

Knowing when to ask for help is part of healthy boundaries.

What support or resources do I need to strengthen my boundary-setting?

TRACING THE TRUTH

THE COMPASS EXERCISE

Boundaries are your internal compass, guiding you toward safety and self-respect. Without it, you can feel adrift in someone else's needs.

Why it helps: This visual metaphor anchors your decision-making, clarifies where your energy should flow, and empowers you to act consistently with your own needs without guilt.

Look at the compass on the next page. "North" represents your emotional limits.
Around the compass, list situations where you felt your limits were crossed.
Identify actions that would honor your *North* without overextending yourself.
Keep the compass visible as a reminder when setting limits in real-life situations.

TRACING THE TRUTH

THE COMPASS EXERCISE

My Emotional Limits

TRACING THE TRUTH

THE GARDEN EXERCISE

Imagine your emotional life as a garden. Boundaries are fences that protect what you want to nurture while keeping weeds of resentment or over-obligation out.

Why it helps:
This exercise translates abstract limits into tangible, visual territory. It reinforces the idea that boundaries aren't punitive—they're protective, nurturing, and essential for growth.

Draw your garden, including spaces that feel overrun or neglected.

Mark areas where boundaries are weak or nonexistent.

List one action for each space to "strengthen the fence" (e.g., saying no, taking time for yourself, delegating tasks).

Check back regularly to see how the garden feels after reinforcing your boundaries.

115

TRACING THE TRUTH

THE GARDEN EXERCISE

TRACING THE TRUTH

THE GARDEN EXERCISE

REFLECTION

TRACING THE TRUTH

THE SHIELD NARRATIVE

Boundaries can feel confrontational or foreign. Reframing them as your shield helps you see them as tools of protection, not aggression.

Why it helps:
Framing boundaries as a protective shield helps reduce guilt by visualizing limits as safety measures rather than rejections, giving you permission to enforce limits with clarity and compassion.

Write a short story where you are a character carrying a shield that represents your emotional limits.
Describe moments where the shield blocks negative energy, prevents overreach, or maintains dignity.
Include moments where you lower the shield intentionally to allow connection that feels safe and reciprocal.
Reflect on how your story mirrors real-life interactions and note small, actionable steps to practice your "shield."

TRACING THE TRUTH

THE SHIELD NARRATIVE

TRACING THE TRUTH

THE SHIELD NARRATIVE

TRACING THE TRUTH

THE SHIELD NARRATIVE

TRACING THE TRUTH

THE SHIELD NARRATIVE

TRACING THE TRUTH

THE SHIELD NARRATIVE

REFLECTION

SAFETY SIGNAL

Our nervous system remembers associations. When you pair a small cue — like a scent, a phrase, or a touch — with calm, it becomes a signal your body can rely on during stressful moments. Over time, encountering the cue can help shift your body from high alert to safety, even when anxiety spikes. This is not magic; it's a gentle, learned shortcut that reminds your brain: I have resources. I can settle. Using this practice regularly strengthens self-regulation and gives you a portable tool for emotional stability.

Choose a cue

Examples include a lavender scent, a short phrase like "I am safe," or a hand on your heart.

Pair with calm

During a relaxed moment, breathe slowly while engaging the cue several times.

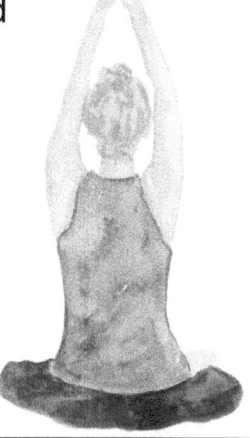

Practice

Repeat this pairing over days until your body notices the association.

Use during spikes

When anxiety rises, bring the cue into awareness while maintaining slow, steady breaths.

Reflect

Notice how your body responds and adjust the cue if needed.

TOUCHSTONE CALM

When anxiety spikes, the body often spirals into future fear or past memories. An anchor object works like a tether to the present moment. The steady texture in your hand gives your nervous system something solid and real to hold onto, cutting through the swirl of anxious thought. Touch is a direct pathway to calming the body — it grounds you without needing words. Over time, simply reaching for your object can become a learned cue of safety and regulation. It's a small, private ritual that says: I am here, I am steady, I am okay.

Choose your object: A smooth stone, piece of jewelry, or small token that feels grounding to touch.

Set intention: Decide: "This is my anchor. It helps me return to now."

Engage the senses: Rub or hold the object, paying attention to its weight, temperature, and texture.

Pair with breath: Inhale slowly, exhale fully as you feel the anchor in your hand.

Practice anywhere: Use during anxious moments, travel, or crowded spaces.

Reinforce: Each time you use it, the association between touch and calm strengthens.

SECTION FIVE

When You've Grown Apart — And You Miss Each Other

There's a kind of loneliness that creeps in even when you're lying in bed next to the person you love. No big betrayal. No massive fight. Just the slow, quiet drift of two people who used to reach for each other without hesitation — now brushing past like polite roommates.

Resentment doesn't always come from what was done wrong. Sometimes it comes from what's missing: affection, effort, enthusiasm. And the ache of that absence — especially when you've tried to name it — can hollow you out.

This section is about the tender work of rebuilding emotional closeness. It's not about forcing connection or faking interest, but gently turning back toward each other with honesty and care. You'll explore where the distance came from, how to express longing without blame, and how to reconnect — even if you're the only one currently reaching. Because sometimes the strongest act of hope is trying again. Not naively — but with boundaries, self-respect, and a willingness to see what's still possible.

Making Sense Of It
The Subtle Erosion of Connection

Emotional drift in long-term relationships often isn't about a single betrayal or failure—it's a quiet, almost imperceptible process that accumulates over time. Neuropsychology shows that the human brain responds powerfully to consistent patterns of attention and validation. In relationships, small acts of recognition—checking in, noticing moods, sharing an inside joke—activate reward pathways, strengthening the sense of safety and connection between partners. When these moments taper off, your brain interprets it almost like a social withdrawal, even if your partner is physically present. You begin to experience the subtle anxiety and melancholy associated with emotional absence, sometimes before you consciously register the distance.

From a sociological and anthropological perspective, the rituals that anchor intimacy—shared meals, playful teasing, collaborative problem-solving—function as cultural glue within a relationship. When these rituals fade, the relationship loses structural scaffolding, and the emotional fabric begins to fray. Even if you remember the early sparks or the promise of shared dreams, your present experience is shaped far more by ongoing, habitual behaviors than by nostalgia. This is why longing for "what was" can coexist with resentment; your emotional system craves the patterns that once signaled care, but those patterns are no longer reliably present.

Attachment theory offers further insight. Secure attachment isn't static; it requires consistent mutual responsiveness.

Making Sense Of It
The Subtle Erosion of Connection

When one or both partners gradually withdraw emotional energy—intentionally or unconsciously—it activates the same neurological circuits that respond to separation or loss. This can lead to heightened vigilance, irritability, or quiet sadness. Importantly, this process is rarely conscious. People rarely drift apart deliberately; it's often the accumulation of small withdrawals, unmet needs, and unspoken disappointments that build the emotional distance.

Cognitive psychology also explains how memory and expectation interact in this process. Your mind naturally recalls times of closeness, amplifying what's missing in the present. This contrast can intensify feelings of loss and longing, even if the relationship is fundamentally stable in other ways. It's not irrational—it's your brain mapping the discrepancy between emotional expectation and reality. And while this mismatch can fuel resentment, it's also a critical signal: it tells you that your needs are not being met, that patterns of communication and connection need conscious attention, and that the emotional health of the relationship depends on intentional engagement rather than passive hope.

Finally, emotional intelligence research highlights the role of curiosity and self-awareness in navigating drift. Recognizing that your longing, disappointment, or frustration is rooted in unmet emotional needs allows you to separate your personal worth from the current state of connection. It also helps you identify actionable pathways: initiating small, honest conversations about distance, inviting shared activities that historically nurtured intimacy, or defining personal boundaries to prevent emotional erosion from becoming self-neglect.

Making Sense Of It
The Subtle Erosion of Connection

By framing distance as a signal rather than a verdict, you shift from reactive blame to proactive repair, giving both partners space to meet each other in a sustainable, grounded way.

Emotional drift is inevitable in many relationships, but awareness, clarity, and intention can transform it from a source of chronic resentment into an opportunity for genuine reconnection. The ache you feel is not a personal failing; it's evidence that your system recognizes the importance of mutual care. By attending to it thoughtfully, you honor both yourself and the relationship, creating conditions where closeness can be rebuilt—or, at the very least, where you can navigate absence with grace, clarity, and self-respect.

Where do I feel the most emotional distance in our relationship?

Identify the areas of disconnect — is it conversation, affection, shared time?

Where do I feel the most emotional distance in our relationship?

What moments of closeness do I miss most?

Reflect on specific memories that made you feel safe, seen, and wanted.

What moments of closeness do I miss most?

When did I start feeling less prioritized or connected?

Understanding the timeline can help uncover root causes.

When did I start feeling less prioritized or connected?

Have I communicated my longing without blame?

Explore whether your expression came from hurt or hope.

Have I communicated my longing without blame?

What fears come up when I consider being vulnerable again?

Resentment often guards pain. Acknowledge what you're protecting.

What fears come up when I consider being vulnerable again?

What have I done to try and repair the distance?

Notice your efforts — and whether they were received or rejected.

What have I done to try and repair the distance?

What does emotional intimacy look like to me now?

It may have changed over time. Define what you truly need.

What does emotional intimacy look like to me now?

If nothing changed, how would I feel a year from now?

Get honest about whether staying emotionally disconnected feels sustainable.

If nothing changed, how would I feel a year from now?

TRACING THE TRUTH

THE ECHO MAP

Emotional drift often leaves you responding to silence or distance without realizing how deeply it affects you. Mapping these echoes helps you understand where connection is missing.

Why it helps:
This exercise makes the invisible patterns visible, helping you see that emotional drift is not random—it's patterned. By identifying the highs and lows, you can respond thoughtfully rather than reactively, and you gain clarity on how to rebuild connection or protect your emotional wellbeing.

Draw a simple outline of your relationship (a line representing "connection" over time).
Mark moments where you felt closeness, warmth, or engagement.
Mark moments where you felt distance, withdrawal, or loneliness.
Reflect and look for patterns: Are there repeated dips? Triggers? Seasons or events where distance grows?

TRACING THE TRUTH

THE ECHO MAP

TRACING THE TRUTH

THE ECHO MAP

REFLECTION

TRACING THE TRUTH

THE SHARED VESSEL

Relationships are like two people holding a shared vessel of care, attention, and energy. When one withdraws, the vessel tilts, and imbalance occurs. This exercise helps you recognize what's actually filling your vessel.

Why it helps:
Visualizing the shared emotional vessel gives tangible insight into imbalance. You see concretely where your efforts go unseen and where connection exists, which empowers you to act from clarity rather than guilt or frustration.

The two overlapping circles represent you and your partner.
Inside your circle, list ways your partner contributes to your sense of connection.

In the overlapping area, list mutual acts of care, support, or shared joy.
Outside the overlap, write what you've been giving that isn't reciprocated.
Reflect on where the vessel is balanced, where it's tilted, and what changes could help restore equilibrium.

TRACING THE TRUTH

THE SHARED VESSEL

TRACING THE TRUTH

THE SHARED VESSEL

REFLECTION

TRACING THE TRUTH

THE SIGNAL LANTERN

Sometimes, we hope our partner will "just notice" when we feel lonely or disconnected. But signals can get lost in drift. This exercise illuminates what you truly need to communicate.

Why it helps:
The Signal Lantern exercise helps you separate your needs from your partner's response. It encourages clarity and self-expression without guilt, and helps you honor your own experience even if the other person isn't fully ready to meet you halfway.

On the next page, there is a lantern representing your emotional voice.
Write down things you wish your partner understood about your experience of distance.
For each, identify the clearest, simplest way to "light the lantern"—how you could communicate it without blame or expectation.
Reflect on whether this communication would be for awareness, not control.

ized

TRACING THE TRUTH

THE SIGNAL LANTERN

**THINGS YOU WISH YOUR
PARTNER UNDERSTOOD**

**HOW YOU COULD LIGHT
THE LANTERN**

TRACING THE TRUTH

THE SIGNAL LANTERN

REFLECTION

SAFETY SIGNAL

Our nervous system remembers associations. When you pair a small cue — like a scent, a phrase, or a touch — with calm, it becomes a signal your body can rely on during stressful moments. Over time, encountering the cue can help shift your body from high alert to safety, even when anxiety spikes. This is not magic; it's a gentle, learned shortcut that reminds your brain: I have resources. I can settle. Using this practice regularly strengthens self-regulation and gives you a portable tool for emotional stability.

Choose a cue

Examples include a lavender scent, a short phrase like "I am safe," or a hand on your heart.

Pair with calm

During a relaxed moment, breathe slowly while engaging the cue several times.

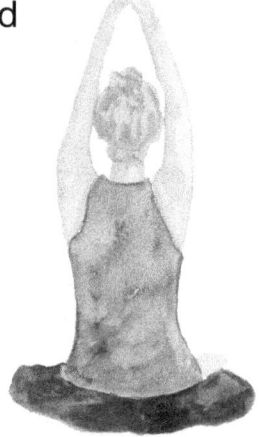

Practice

Repeat this pairing over days until your body notices the association.

Use during spikes

When anxiety rises, bring the cue into awareness while maintaining slow, steady breaths.

Reflect

Notice how your body responds and adjust the cue if needed.

TOUCHSTONE CALM

When anxiety spikes, the body often spirals into future fear or past memories. An anchor object works like a tether to the present moment. The steady texture in your hand gives your nervous system something solid and real to hold onto, cutting through the swirl of anxious thought. Touch is a direct pathway to calming the body — it grounds you without needing words. Over time, simply reaching for your object can become a learned cue of safety and regulation. It's a small, private ritual that says: I am here, I am steady, I am okay.

Choose your object: A smooth stone, piece of jewelry, or small token that feels grounding to touch.

Set intention: Decide: "This is my anchor. It helps me return to now."

Engage the senses: Rub or hold the object, paying attention to its weight, temperature, and texture.

Pair with breath: Inhale slowly, exhale fully as you feel the anchor in your hand.

Practice anywhere: Use during anxious moments, travel, or crowded spaces.

Reinforce: Each time you use it, the association between touch and calm strengthens.

SECTION SIX

When You Feel Like You're Always the One Trying

It's exhausting to feel like the only one holding things together. When you're the one reading books like this, initiating hard conversations, and trying to do the emotional labor for two people, resentment can build quietly but powerfully. You start asking yourself: Why am I the only one trying? And it's not just about logistics or fairness — it's about feeling unseen. Unmet in the places that matter most.

This section is here to help you recognize that emotional imbalance without automatically jumping to blame or helplessness. It's about understanding the invisible workload that comes with caretaking, people-pleasing, or simply loving deeply — and finding a new way to move forward without burning out or building more walls. We're going to take a closer look at the mental load, emotional invisibility, and how to communicate your need for effort without keeping score — because you deserve a relationship where you aren't always running on empty.

Making Sense Of It
The Invisible Ledger

Sometimes, effort isn't measured by gestures, words, or grand declarations — it's measured in the quiet, daily labor of being attuned to someone else's moods, needs, and unspoken expectations. When that labor is one-sided, it doesn't just leave you tired; it reshapes your nervous system. Neuroscience shows that chronic caretaking and emotional overextension activate stress pathways in the body — elevated cortisol, tension in the chest, tight shoulders, and fatigue — even when the imbalance is largely invisible to others. You aren't imagining the heaviness. Your body remembers every unreciprocated effort, every unanswered question, every time you stretched to fill the emotional gap.

Anthropology teaches us that humans evolved to navigate social hierarchies and reciprocal care. When reciprocity breaks down — when you're consistently the one giving while the other withdraws — the brain interprets it as social threat. It triggers vigilance, hyper-awareness, and subtle anxiety: the same systems that kept our ancestors safe in unpredictable environments now keep you awake at night over things that "shouldn't" feel this heavy. Your heart and mind are not failing you; they're responding to a chronic, relational stressor that your social and emotional instincts were designed to detect.

Emotionally, this imbalance also erodes self-perception. Sociological research on relational equity shows that people in over-functioning roles often internalize responsibility for the relationship's success. You may find yourself constantly monitoring your partner's reactions, measuring your own worth by their engagement, and doubting your intuition when needs are unmet.

Making Sense Of It
The Invisible Ledger

Over time, this rewires the emotional landscape: resentment grows quietly, hope is tethered to effort rather than mutual care, and authenticity is sacrificed for the illusion of connection.

The paradox is brutal: the more you try to preserve the relationship, the more exhausted you become, and the less energy remains for self-preservation. But understanding this is empowering. Recognizing the biological, sociological, and emotional mechanisms behind "always trying" doesn't excuse imbalance — it clarifies it. It allows you to see your own energy as finite, your effort as valuable, and your boundaries as not just reasonable but necessary. Healing isn't about stopping care entirely; it's about recalibrating effort so that it aligns with what's sustainable and reciprocated, protecting your nervous system, your heart, and your identity.

By naming the invisible weight you carry and understanding why it impacts your mind, body, and relationships, you can start making conscious choices: where to invest effort, where to step back, and where to demand reciprocity without guilt. You can begin to untangle love from labor, presence from overextension, and care from self-erasure. It's not an instant fix, but insight is the first step toward reclaiming your energy, your voice, and your sense of safety in relationships that are meant to nourish you — not drain you.

Where do I feel most alone in the effort to make this relationship better?

Describe the situations where you feel like you're the only one who notices, initiates, or cares.

Where do I feel most alone in the effort to make this relationship better?

How do I communicate my needs — clearly or through burnout?

Explore whether you're expressing needs directly or hoping your exhaustion will speak for itself.

How do I communicate my needs — clearly or through burnout?

What are the small ways I keep this relationship going that often go unnoticed?

Make a list — even the smallest things — so you can see how much you're carrying.

What are the small ways I keep this relationship going that often go unnoticed?

What kind of effort would help me feel emotionally safe and met?

Name specific actions or shifts that would make you feel like your partner is showing up too.

What kind of effort would help me feel emotionally safe and met?

When I express my hurt, do I leave room for my partner's humanity?

Reflect on whether you're communicating in a way that invites empathy or defensiveness.

When I express my hurt, do I leave room for my partner's humanity?

What would it mean for me to stop over-functioning in this relationship?

This is a hard one. What would change — in you, in them, in the dynamic?

What would it mean for me to stop over-functioning in this relationship?

Do I equate love with effort — and does that sometimes blur into resentment?

Notice if being the "fixer" gives you identity or control that might be masking deeper needs.

Do I equate love with effort — and does that sometimes blur into resentment?

What version of "us" am I trying to preserve — and is it actually working for me?

Be honest about whether the relationship you're working so hard to protect still reflects what you want.

What version of "us" am I trying to preserve — and is it actually working for me?

TRACING THE TRUTH

MAPPING THE INVISIBLE LOAD

You can't manage what you can't see. Mapping your emotional labor gives form to what often feels invisible, helping you understand where your energy goes.

Why it helps:
Visualizing the invisible labor clarifies the scope of the imbalance, reduces self-blame, and helps you see where boundaries or recalibration are needed.

Look at the two columns on the next page. Label one "Effort I Give" and the other "Effort I Receive."

List daily and weekly actions in the "Effort I Give" column — from listening, planning, checking in, to emotional support.

In the "Effort I Receive" column, note moments your partner reciprocates — however small.

Reflect and observe the imbalance without judgment.

TRACING THE TRUTH

MAPPING THE INVISIBLE LOAD

Effort I Give

Effort I Receive

TRACING THE TRUTH

MAPPING THE INVISIBLE LOAD

REFLECTION

TRACING THE TRUTH

THE ENERGY RESERVOIR

Your emotional energy is like water in a reservoir. If you pour it all out into one channel without replenishment, the reservoir runs dry.

Why it helps:
This exercise externalizes your energy flow, showing where you overextend. It encourages conscious allocation of effort and prioritizes self-care to prevent emotional burnout.

The rectangle represents a reservoir, your reservoir.
Shade or fill in sections for where your emotional energy is currently spent: work, family, partner, personal care.
Identify areas where you are overpouring and areas left empty.
Write actions you can take this week to refill your reservoir.

TRACING THE TRUTH

THE ENERGY RESERVOIR

TRACING THE TRUTH

THE ENERGY RESERVOIR

REFLECTION

TRACING THE TRUTH

THE STRINGS YOU CARRY

Being the only one trying can feel like carrying invisible strings — tension that tugs at your heart and mind constantly. Naming these strings allows you to gently release what isn't yours to bear.

Why it helps:
Physically visualizing emotional strings externalizes the tension and empowers you to decide what to carry and what to release, reducing invisible labor and reclaiming autonomy.

The figure on the next page represents you.
From your figure, draw lines for each ongoing effort or emotional responsibility you feel toward the relationship.
Label each string (e.g., "reminding them of plans," "soothing tension," "adjusting my schedule").
For each string, reflect and ask: "Do I choose to carry this? Or is this responsibility theirs?" Draw scissors next to strings you decide to release.

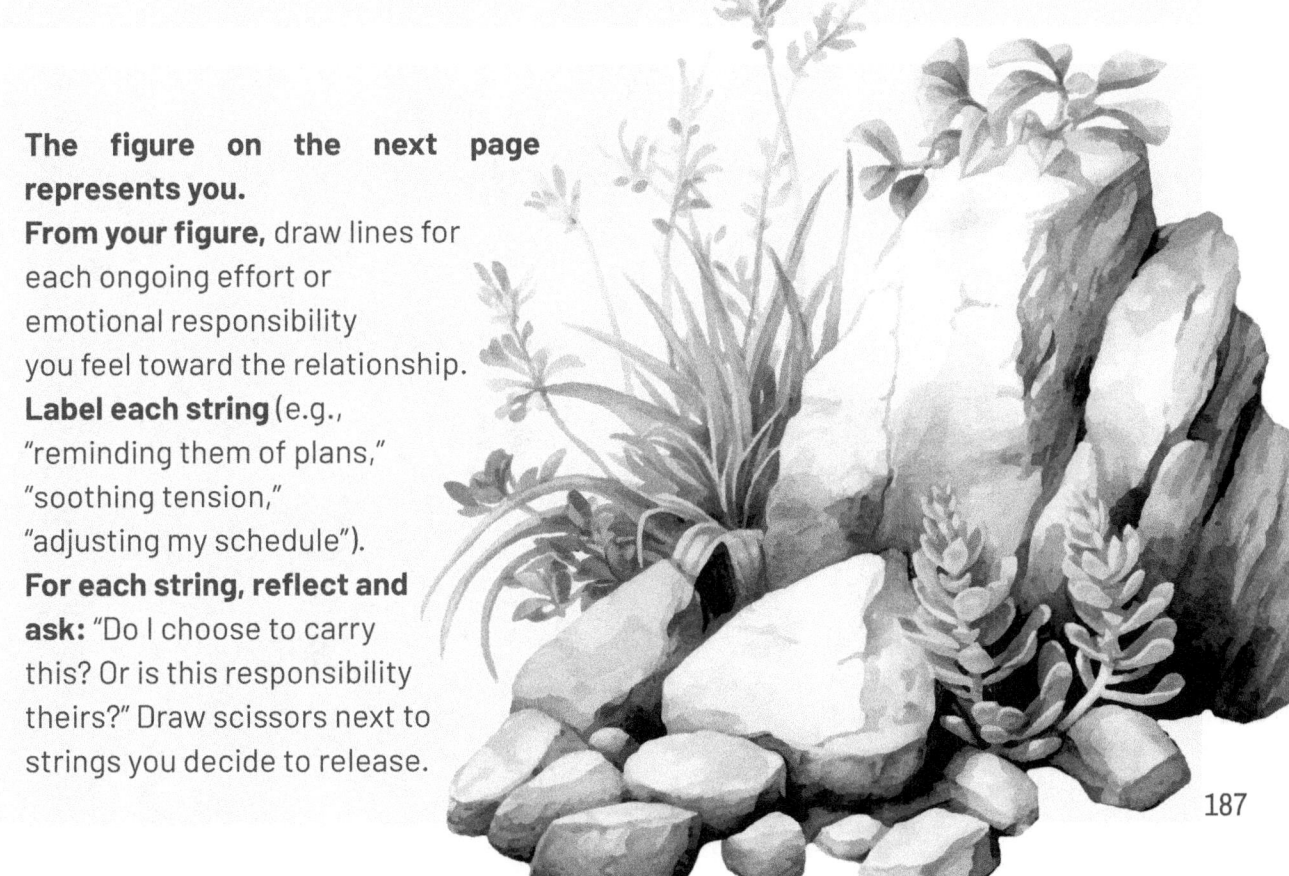

TRACING THE TRUTH

THE STRINGS YOU CARRY

TRACING THE TRUTH

THE STRINGS YOU CARRY

REFLECTION

THE 5-4-3-2-1 RESET

When anxiety floods you, your brain hijacks the moment with "what ifs." This tool cuts through spirals by anchoring you in your body's real-time experience. It reactivates the sensory pathways, pulling you out of mental overdrive and into the safety of the present moment. Instead of fighting thoughts, you drop into your senses — a place your nervous system recognizes as grounding.

When your mind is racing or panic takes over, gently bring yourself back through your senses. You can do this out loud, in a whisper, or in your head. Take your time and make sure you really notice what you're observing slowly.

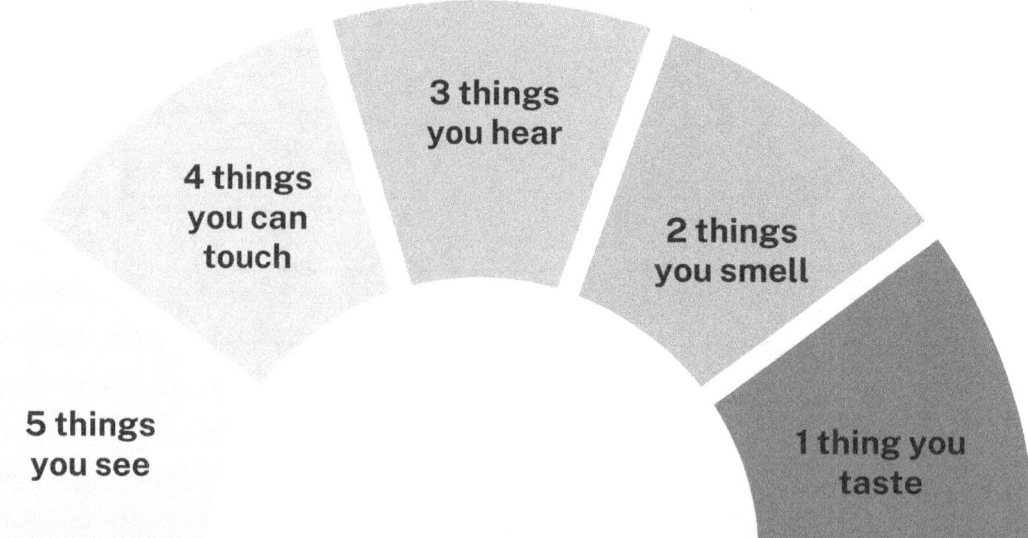

THE BREATH SQUARE

When anxiety floods you, your brain hijacks the moment with "what ifs." This tool cuts through spirals by anchoring you in your body's real-time experience. It reactivates the sensory pathways, pulling you out of mental overdrive and into the safety of the present moment. Instead of fighting thoughts, you drop into your senses — a place your nervous system recognizes as grounding.

Inhale for 4 as you trace the first side.

Hold for 4 as you trace the next side.

Exhale for 4 as you trace the third side.

Hold for 4 as you complete the square.

> **Repeat this cycle 3–5 times.** Keep your pace steady — not too fast, not too slow. Imagine you're sketching calm into the air with each breath.

SECTION SEVEN

Resentment or Realism — When It Feels Like You're Always Giving More

There's a specific kind of ache that comes from feeling like the one who always tries harder. The one who plans the date nights, keeps the emotional pulse of the relationship, holds space, initiates the hard talks, remembers the birthdays, diffuses the fights. And maybe you've convinced yourself it's fine — "someone has to" — but underneath, it stings. It builds. And eventually, that sting becomes resentment.

But what if we asked a different question: Is your resentment pointing to an unmet need, or is it pointing to a lopsided reality? Because not all resentment is a story you're telling yourself. Sometimes it's a signal — an alarm bell that you've become the over-functioning one in a relationship that's emotionally underfed. This section isn't about blaming your partner or gaslighting yourself into gratitude. It's about naming what's real, owning your limits, and learning to respond with clarity instead of collapse. And if you've been the burnt toast person — the one always settling for the coldest plate — we're about to rewrite that.

Making Sense Of It
When Effort Becomes Currency

There's a subtle mental shift that happens when giving in a relationship becomes habitual rather than mutual. Over time, the brain begins to normalize the imbalance — a phenomenon sociologists and psychologists sometimes call "role entrenchment." Your brain starts encoding a pattern: "I am the giver; they are the receiver." This isn't moral failure or weakness — it's adaptive wiring. Evolutionarily, humans were wired to maintain social bonds even when effort wasn't immediately reciprocated, because survival often depended on cooperation. But what once helped communities thrive can, in the microcosm of a two-person relationship, quietly erode your sense of self.

Neuroscience shows that chronic overgiving activates the brain's stress response, particularly the amygdala, in ways similar to threat or danger. When your emotional labor consistently outweighs what you receive, your body interprets it as a prolonged state of vigilance. This can manifest as tension in the chest, shallow breathing, disrupted sleep, or a low-level, persistent irritability. The emotional cost is not abstract; it's physiological, shaping your moods, your energy, and even your capacity to feel joy. Your resentment is not a moral flaw — it's your nervous system signaling that your boundaries are being breached.

Anthropologically, humans also carry a strong reciprocity bias. Across cultures, we are conditioned to match investment in relationships with the returns we receive — emotionally, materially, or socially. When that balance fails repeatedly, our minds struggle to reconcile effort with outcome. That mismatch fuels a creeping sense of unfairness, which psychologists term equity distress.

Making Sense Of It
When Effort Becomes Currency

You may find yourself apologizing for frustration, excusing behavior that hurts you, or minimizing your own needs to preserve the connection. These are all understandable survival strategies — ways your mind has learned to cope with imbalance — but they also deepen the quiet erosion of self-worth.

Emotionally, resentment often masquerades as anger, sadness, or irritability, but its roots are pragmatic and relational, not irrational. It is an emotional compass pointing straight to unmet needs. And here's the critical insight: recognizing this doesn't require moral judgment or self-recrimination. It requires clarity — a willingness to separate your feelings from the story you tell yourself about them. Resentment is neither "bad" nor "wrong." It is data. It tells you exactly where the scales are off, where your energy is being extracted, and where boundaries have dissolved without consent.

Understanding this is also sociologically profound. Studies of relational labor — the emotional and logistical work people perform in partnerships — show that women and emotionally attuned individuals disproportionately carry this load, often invisibly. The social expectation to prioritize care and emotional management compounds the personal cost. Being the "over-functioning" partner doesn't mean you are weak; it means you are responding to a social script and learned patterns of attachment — often from childhood — that train you to value others' needs over your own.

Making Sense Of It
When Effort Becomes Currency

So how do we translate insight into action? It starts with seeing your resentment as a mirror, not a weapon. It is the mind's way of reflecting unmet needs back to you in clear, if uncomfortable, terms. Paying attention, naming it, and tracing it to specific unmet needs or repeated imbalances allows you to respond with agency rather than reactivity. This is where realism enters: you can honor your effort, acknowledge your fatigue, and discern what is yours to carry — and what belongs to the other person. That discernment is the beginning of reclaiming your energy, your clarity, and your emotional integrity.

In essence, resentment and realism are siblings. One whispers, "I am tired of carrying this alone." The other replies, "This is what is true right now. What choices do I have?" The healthiest path lies in listening to both, interpreting the signals of your body and mind, and responding from awareness rather than habit. Resentment isn't a failure — it's intelligence. And once you understand its message, you can start reshaping your relationship with yourself, your partner, and the effort you bring into your life.

Where have I been silently accepting the 'burnt toast' in this relationship?

What patterns have I normalized that actually leave me feeling undervalued?

Where have I been silently accepting the 'burnt toast' in this relationship?

When I picture asking for more, what feelings come up?

Explore whether it's fear, guilt, shame, or something else — and where that comes from.

When I picture asking for more, what feelings come up?

Have I convinced myself that my partner just "doesn't get it"?

Unpack whether this belief is keeping you from communicating clearly or asking for what you need.

Have I convinced myself that my partner just "doesn't get it"?

How do I define 'pulling my weight' in a relationship — and does my partner see it the same way?

Look at emotional labor, logistics, and how effort is distributed.

How do I define 'pulling my weight' in a relationship — and does my partner see it the same way?

What stories have I told myself to justify accepting less than I deserve?

Sometimes resentment is tied to an outdated narrative — what's yours?

What stories have I told myself to justify accepting less than I deserve?

How do I want to feel in a relationship — day to day?

Ground this in emotion, not fantasy. Peaceful? Seen? Respected?

How do I want to feel in a relationship — day to day?

What would it mean to stop overfunctioning — and how might that change the relationship dynamic?

Reflect on what you fear would happen if you stopped doing it all.

What would it mean to stop overfunctioning — and how might that change the relationship dynamic?

Have I clearly named what I want — or just dropped hints and hoped they'd catch on?

Resentment often builds in the silence between what we need and what we say.

Have I clearly named what I want — or just dropped hints and hoped they'd catch on?

TRACING THE TRUTH

THE "ENERGY LEDGER"

Resentment often builds silently because we track effort in our heads, not on paper. This exercise makes it tangible.

Why it helps:
Seeing your contributions versus what's returned clarifies whether resentment comes from unmet needs or distorted expectations. It externalizes the imbalance so you can respond consciously instead of unconsciously burning out.

For one week, write down moments of effort, emotional labor, or attention you put into the relationship in the left column.

In the right column, record what you received in return — gestures, support, or acknowledgment.

Reflect at the end of the week: notice patterns, gaps, and moments of reciprocity.

TRACING THE TRUTH

THE "ENERGY LEDGER"

What I Give	What I Receive

TRACING THE TRUTH

THE "ENERGY LEDGER"

What I Give	What I Receive

TRACING THE TRUTH

THE "ENERGY LEDGER"

REFLECTION

TRACING THE TRUTH

THE "BOUNDARY GARDEN"

Resentment grows when boundaries are ignored or unclear. Treat your emotional limits like plants in a garden.

Why it helps:
Visualizing boundaries as living things reinforces that they need care, attention, and respect — yours and others' — to thrive. It shifts the mindset from guilt to stewardship of your emotional space.

Label each plant in the garden as a boundary you want to protect (time, energy, emotional space).

For each boundary, write what nurtures it (e.g., saying no, asking for support) and what weeds it (e.g., over-apologizing, ignoring your needs).

Write one simple but concrete action you can do to "water" one of your boundaries.

TRACING THE TRUTH

THE "BOUNDARY GARDEN"

Name your Boundaries

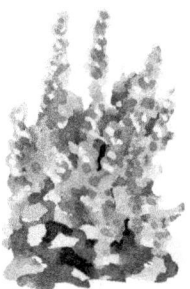

TRACING THE TRUTH

THE "BOUNDARY GARDEN"

Boundary:

How to Nurture it:

Action to Try:

Boundary:

How to Nurture it:

Action to Try:

Boundary:

How to Nurture it:

Action to Try:

TRACING THE TRUTH

THE "BOUNDARY GARDEN"

Boundary:

How to Nurture it:

Action to Try:

Boundary:

How to Nurture it:

Action to Try:

Boundary:

How to Nurture it:

Action to Try:

TRACING THE TRUTH

THE "RESENTMENT MAP"

Resentment can feel amorphous and overwhelming. Mapping it out gives structure and perspective.

Why it helps:
This exercise translates abstract resentment into clear emotional signals. It helps you see the root needs, differentiate between perception and reality, and take agency in addressing your own wellbeing.

Around the circle, draw lines to each source of resentment in your relationship. Label them (e.g., "Unacknowledged effort," "Missed promises").
On each line, note the feelings that arise (anger, sadness, exhaustion) and the needs underneath them.
Identify one small step you could take to honor that need — without expecting the other person to change.

TRACING THE TRUTH

THE "RESENTMENT MAP"

CRISIS PAUSE

When emotions run high, it's easy to get pulled into extremes—either reacting purely from feelings or overthinking with logic alone. Wise Mind Access helps you pause and bring both sides together: your emotional insight and your reasoned perspective. By visualizing Emotion Mind and Reasonable Mind meeting, you create space for clarity, calm, and grounded decision-making. Writing down the first calm thought that arises captures the guidance of your "middle path," helping you respond intentionally rather than reacting impulsively.

STEP 1
Stop.

Freeze for a beat. Don't send the text, don't make the call, don't decide. Hands still.

STEP 2
Take a step back.

One slow breath or a literal step backward. Say quietly, "Pause."

STEP 3
Observe.

Notice: What's happening in my body? What are the facts (not the story)? What's my goal? What's in my control right now? (This is your Reasonable Mind check.)

STEP 4
Proceed mindfully.

Pick one effective action that serves your goal—something small, safe, and workable (e.g., "wait 10 minutes," "use a calm script," "walk to the sink and drink water"). Follow through.

SPEAK & STAY STEADY

When emotions run high, it's easy to either go silent or come in too strong. DEAR MAN gives you a clear framework for making requests—or saying no—without guilt or aggression. It balances honesty with effectiveness so you can be heard and respected, even in difficult conversations.

Describe

Briefly state the facts. ("Last week, you didn't follow through on picking up the kids.")

Express

Share how it impacted you. ("I felt really stressed and overwhelmed.")

Assert

Clearly ask for what you need. ("I need you to confirm pick-up times in advance.")

Reinforce

Show the positive outcome. ("That way, we both have more peace of mind.")

Mindful

Stay on point; don't chase distractions or get pulled into side arguments.

Appear confident

Sit up, steady tone, eye contact if possible. Confidence helps your words land.

Negotiate

Be flexible; invite collaboration. ("If that time doesn't work, let's pick another together.")

Making Sense Of It
Choosing Your Battles to Protect Your Peace

Resentment accumulates like sediment in a riverbed. Tiny grievances, small disappointments, and overlooked efforts settle quietly, layer by layer, until they form a weight that drags your heart downstream. It's not the single missed text or forgotten promise that breaks you — it's the constant layering of minor injuries that keeps your nervous system in a low hum of tension.

Your body remembers imbalance even when your mind tries to rationalize it. Muscles tighten, stomachs churn, sleep fragments. Psychology tells us that chronic low-level stress from relational imbalance triggers a fight-or-flight response over and over, making even small slights feel amplified. This is why you feel drained, anxious, or reactive without knowing why — your system is perpetually bracing for impact.

Deciding what deserves your attention is a skill of survival. Emotional energy is finite, and your wellbeing depends on preserving it. Not every irritation is a signal to act; some are noise. Sociologists note that humans naturally catalogue slights to track fairness and reciprocity, but in one-sided relationships this instinct backfires, trapping you in cycles of imagined grievance. Choosing your battles isn't ignoring reality — it's identifying the moments that truly affect your dignity, safety, and emotional balance.

When you release the small stuff, you reclaim relational bandwidth. Anthropology shows that in communities with long-term social cohesion, members survive and thrive because they conserve energy for conflicts that genuinely matter.

Making Sense Of It
Choosing Your Battles to Protect Your Peace

Translating this to your life means letting minor frustrations dissolve instead of letting them fester. Each act of letting go is a signal to yourself: your attention is precious, your emotional safety matters, and peace is not negotiable.

This practice reshapes your internal landscape. It creates room for empathy, presence, and clarity, instead of chronic irritability and resentment. The quiet moments between choosing and letting go build a subtle muscle: the ability to engage deeply when necessary, and to protect yourself when it's not. Over time, these choices form a relational architecture where your energy is honored, your heart is safeguarded, and your capacity for meaningful connection expands.

Ultimately, protecting your peace is an act of radical self-respect. It's saying to yourself that not every moment is worth the fight, that your nervous system deserves relief, and that the quality of your attention — to yourself and others — defines the quality of your life. Choosing your battles doesn't shrink your love; it sharpens your clarity and frees your heart to focus where it can truly flourish.

What are the "small things" I find myself replaying or resenting the most?

Identify patterns in your irritation. What truly matters, and what might be noise?

What are the "small things" I find myself replaying or resenting the most?

How does focusing on minor annoyances affect my mood and interactions?

Reflect on the cost of carrying these little resentments.

How does focusing on minor annoyances affect my mood and interactions?

When was the last time I let go of a small frustration and felt relief?

Recall moments when releasing control helped you breathe easier.

When was the last time I let go of a small frustration and felt relief?

What fears come up when I think about ignoring or releasing these little slights?

Explore if you worry letting go means accepting less or being vulnerable.

What fears come up when I think about ignoring or releasing these little slights?

How can I tell the difference between small stuff and important issues?

Define your own boundaries around what deserves your emotional bandwidth.

How can I tell the difference between small stuff and important issues?

What would my relationship look like if I saved energy for the big things?

Visualize the space and calm that could come from less reactive energy.

What would my relationship look like if I saved energy for the big things?

How can practicing letting go benefit my mental and emotional health?

Connect the dots between release and self-care.

How can practicing letting go benefit my mental and emotional health?

What small steps can I take this week to practice not sweating the small stuff?

Brainstorm realistic, concrete actions.

What small steps can I take this week to practice not sweating the small stuff?

TRACING THE TRUTH

THE PEBBLE VS. BOULDER LIST

Not every slight deserves your energy. Some are pebbles you can let slide; others are boulders that demand attention. This exercise helps you sort what really matters.

Why it helps:
This exercise externalizes internal noise, giving you clarity on where to spend your emotional energy. It trains your nervous system to focus on what truly matters, reducing burnout and quieting constant tension.

On the next page, write down recent moments that triggered irritation, frustration, or resentment.
Label each as either a "Pebble" (small, manageable, let go) or a "Boulder" (impactful, boundary-crossing, needs response).
Reflect on why each item earned its label.

TRACING THE TRUTH

THE PEBBLE VS. BOULDER LIST

Pebbles

Boulders

TRACING THE TRUTH

THE PEBBLE VS. BOULDER LIST

REFLECTION

TRACING THE TRUTH

EMOTIONAL BANK BALANCE

Every interaction draws on your emotional reserves. This exercise lets you track deposits and withdrawals, helping you see when you're overextended.

Why it helps:
Tracking emotional labor visually makes imbalance concrete. It reveals where resentment may be forming and empowers you to protect your energy, choosing engagement intentionally rather than reactively.

Fill out the table on the next page.
List recent interactions that cost you emotionally.
Note whether the energy spent felt replenishing, neutral, or draining.
Reflect and identify patterns: Are certain types of interactions always draining? Are some consistently replenishing?

TRACING THE TRUTH

EMOTIONAL BANK BALANCE

Interaction	Energy Spent	Emotional Outcome

TRACING THE TRUTH

EMOTIONAL BANK BALANCE

Interaction	Energy Spent	Emotional Outcome

250

TRACING THE TRUTH

EMOTIONAL BANK BALANCE

REFLECTION

PRACTICE PEACE

When you anticipate a challenging moment—whether it's a tense conversation, an overwhelming task, or a triggering situation—your mind can spiral with worry or panic. Cope Ahead lets you practice calm responses before the moment hits. By imagining the scenario in detail and rehearsing coping strategies, you train your nervous system to respond more skillfully. Even if things go sideways, visualizing recovery reduces shame, panic, and self-blame. This exercise builds confidence and a sense of preparedness so you feel more grounded in real life.

Identify the upcoming challenge. Pick a situation that usually triggers strong emotions.
Visualize in detail. Imagine the setting, who's there, what's being said, and how you normally feel.
Rehearse coping skills. Step through the strategies you want to use—breathing, grounding, assertive statements, or self-soothing actions.
Visualize recovery. Picture what you'll do if things go differently than planned, focusing on calm, steady responses.
Reflect and write. Note any adjustments or insights you gained from the rehearsal.

Anticipated Situation

Coping Steps Rehearsed	Recovery Plan / Visualize Success

MOMENTS OF LIGHT

When life feels heavy, it's easy to overlook the small, positive moments that actually keep us grounded. Intentionally creating and noticing positive experiences rewires your brain to notice what feels good, rather than only what feels wrong. Over time, these moments build momentum, helping you feel more resilient, connected, and capable. Short-term enjoyment strengthens your nervous system's sense of safety; long-term, value-aligned actions help you create a life that genuinely feels worth living.

Schedule small joys daily

Pick one tiny thing each day that sparks a little happiness—coffee in silence, a walk, listening to music, a funny video.

Record the experience

Write down how it felt in the moment.

Plan one value-aligned action per week

Something bigger that aligns with your goals or values—reaching out to a friend, pursuing a hobby, volunteering.

Reflect on impact

Notice shifts in mood, energy, or perspective after small and larger actions.

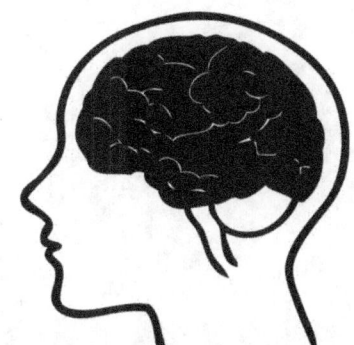

Repeat consistently

Gradually, these small and larger positive moments accumulate to create lasting emotional lift.

SECTION EIGHT

When Letting Go Means Finding Peace, Not Giving Up

Letting go is one of those phrases that sounds simple but feels almost impossible when your heart is tangled up in resentment. It's not about giving up on the relationship or pretending everything's fine. It's about creating a space inside yourself where peace is possible — whether your partner is ready to meet you there or not.

Holding on to resentment feels like carrying a heavy backpack everywhere you go. It shapes how you see your partner, the relationship, even yourself. But holding on tight doesn't protect you — it hurts you. Learning to release some of that weight is a radical act of self-care. It's saying to yourself, "I deserve peace, even if this isn't perfect."

This section will help you understand why letting go is for you first, and how to find calm in the chaos, so resentment stops running the show — no matter what your partner does.

Making Sense Of It
Letting Go as a Practice of Self-Claim

Resentment is tricky. It disguises itself as protection, whispering that holding on will shield you from pain. But over time, it becomes a weight tethered to your chest, a constant hum in your nervous system, shaping how you think, feel, and even move through the world. It isn't just a thought—you can feel it in your body: the tight shoulders, the pit in your stomach, the way your energy feels drained before the day has even started. Neuroscience shows that chronic anger and rumination keep the amygdala on high alert, triggering stress responses that wear down both mind and body.

We are wired to notice imbalance. Anthropologists and sociologists remind us that humans evolved to track fairness and reciprocity; in small social groups, this was survival. In a relationship, noticing who gives and who takes is part of that wiring. But when you're always the one giving, your mind interprets the imbalance as a personal failing—even when it isn't. Emotional intelligence teaches us that naming this pattern without blame is the first step toward breaking the cycle, because resentment is often less about the other person and more about the energy we are giving away without return.

Letting go doesn't mean ignoring harm or pretending it didn't happen. Psychology calls this cognitive reappraisal: the process of choosing how you interpret events to protect your sense of self while holding truth in your heart. When you release resentment, you're not giving up on accountability—you're reclaiming your energy. You're moving the locus of control from someone else's choices back to your own.

Making Sense Of It
Letting Go as a Practice of Self-Claim

This is radical self-sovereignty in action.
Holding onto resentment reshapes perception. Small annoyances feel magnified, and your partner is seen less as a human being and more as a catalog of unmet needs. Letting go, by contrast, clears space for nuance. You can act instead of react, communicate instead of withdrawing, and engage without being weighed down by past hurts.

Self-compassion is part of this process. Letting go is a message to yourself: your emotional experience matters more than the injustices of another. Positive psychology shows that self-compassion strengthens resilience, helps regulate emotion, and builds the boundaries that keep relationships healthier. Releasing resentment doesn't mean excusing bad behavior—it means honoring your own inner life.

Finally, think of letting go not as surrender, but as creating space. Peace isn't about erasing reality or pretending everything is fine—it's a state of safety and clarity, rooted in choice. When resentment softens, your nervous system relaxes, your heart opens, and your mind has room to focus on what matters: connection, clarity, and your own sense of agency. Letting go is a daily practice, a deliberate reclaiming of your power, a way to carry your heart without carrying the weight of accumulated anger. It is an act of courage, self-respect, and love—for yourself first, and for the possibility of better connection second.

What would peace look like for me, regardless of what my partner does?

Visualize what inner calm feels like without relying on external change.

What would peace look like for me, regardless of what my partner does?

When I hold on to resentment, what am I protecting myself from?

Identify the fears or beliefs that keep you stuck.

When I hold on to resentment, what am I protecting myself from?

How has resentment impacted my health, mood, or behavior?

Notice the real costs of carrying this weight daily.

How has resentment impacted my health, mood, or behavior?

What parts of the relationship can I accept as they are, without needing to fix?

Explore where acceptance can create space for peace.

What parts of the relationship can I accept as they are, without needing to fix?

What small steps can I take today to practice letting go?

Think about concrete actions or mindset shifts.

What small steps can I take today to practice letting go?

How can I remind myself that letting go is about me first, not them?

Develop personal affirmations or rituals.

How can I remind myself that letting go is about me first, not them?

What boundaries do I need to set to protect my peace?

Outline what feels safe and sustainable moving forward.

What boundaries do I need to set to protect my peace?

How will my life improve if resentment no longer controls my reactions?

Imagine the freedom and energy that will open up.

How will my life improve if resentment no longer controls my reactions?

TRACING THE TRUTH

THE BACKPACK CHECK-IN

Resentment often feels like a backpack full of rocks you've been carrying everywhere. Some are obvious, some hidden. This exercise helps you identify what you're actually carrying—and decide what to keep and what to set down.

Why it helps:
Resentment often feels like a backpack full of rocks you've been carrying everywhere. Some are obvious, some hidden. This exercise helps you identify what you're actually carrying—and decide what to keep and what to set down.

Take a quiet moment with paper and pen.

The backpack on the next page represents what you carry emotionally.

Draw and label "rocks" inside with resentments, grudges, or lingering frustrations you've been holding onto.

For each rock, ask yourself: Is this mine to carry? Does holding it protect me or hurt me?

Draw a "release zipper" and list which rocks you are ready to set down.

275

TRACING THE TRUTH

THE BACKPACK CHECK-IN

TRACING THE TRUTH

THE COMPASS OF CONTROL

Resentment often grows when we focus on what we can't change. This exercise turns your attention to what is actually within your control, helping you redirect energy where it matters.

Why it helps:
Shifting focus from external outcomes to internal agency reduces rumination. Neuroscience shows that feeling in control of even small choices lowers stress and opens space for healthier relational engagement.

Use the compass on the next page.
Label the north: *Things I cannot control.* List your partner's choices, moods, and reactions here.
Label the south: Things I can control. Include your actions, responses, and boundaries.
Circle or highlight the items in the south and consider one practical action you can take today.

TRACING THE TRUTH

THE COMPASS OF CONTROL

THE TRIGGER MAP

When you react automatically, it often feels like there's no pause between what happens and how you respond. This exercise helps you slow things down and see the chain of events clearly—what triggered the feeling, the thought that popped up, the urge, and what actually happened. Once you can see it all laid out, you can spot the point where you can intervene next time. That small pause is enough to change the outcome, give yourself more control, and break patterns that have been running on autopilot.

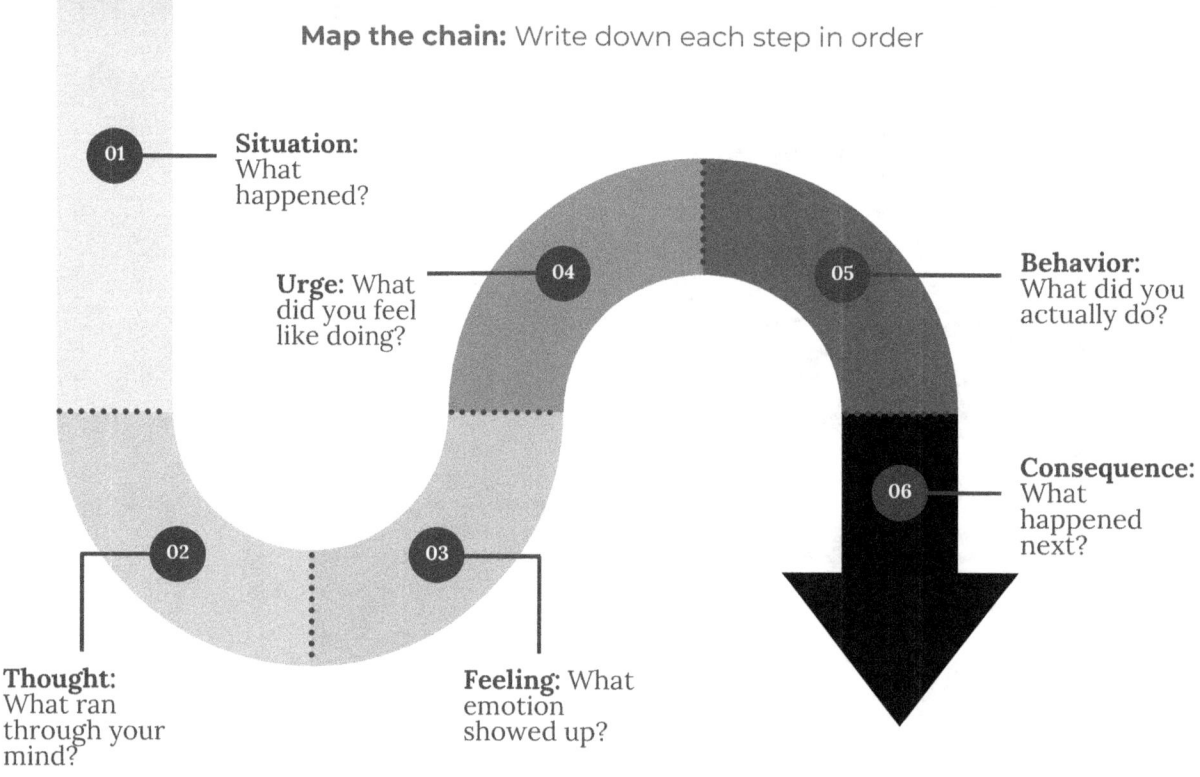

Circle your change point. Look at the chain and find the first step where you could intervene next time.

Plan one interruption. Pick a tool or skill to use—like a short breathing exercise, a script you can say, or a grounding move—to pause the chain and respond differently.

CLIMBING DOWN

When your mind hits you with a brutal thought—like "I always mess up"—it can feel impossible to jump straight to a positive or kind belief. Your brain just won't buy it. This exercise gives you a middle ground. By writing the harsh thought at the top and gradually stepping down to gentler, more realistic versions, you give yourself space to find a statement that actually feels believable. Even if it's not perfect, that 70% believable thought is enough to lower the intensity and guide you toward calmer choices today.

Write the harsh thought at the top rung. (e.g., "I always mess up.")
Step down slowly. Each rung is a slightly softer, more balanced version of the thought.
> "I mess up sometimes, but not always."
> "Everyone makes mistakes. Mine don't erase the things I do well."
> "I can learn from this and try again."

Pick the rung that feels about 70% true. You don't have to land at the bottom. Just stop where it feels believable.
Act from that rung. Let today's choices come from this steadier, more grounded statement.

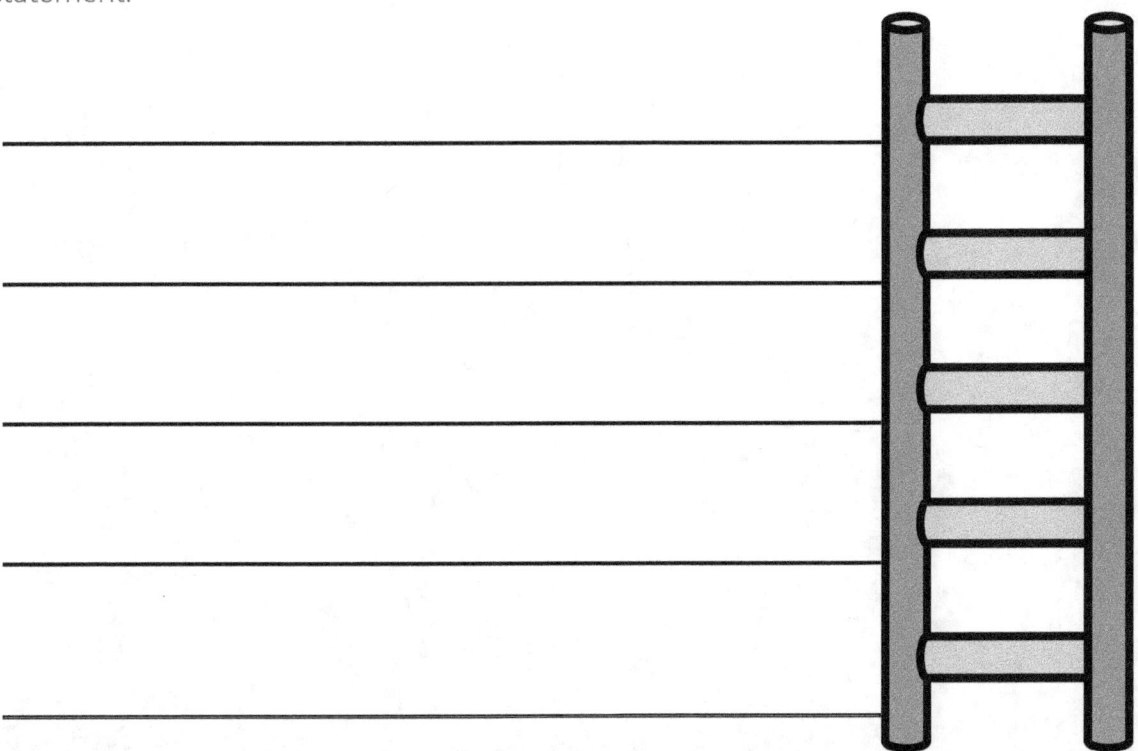

SECTION NINE

The Echoes Around You — How Outside Forces Shape Your Resentment

No relationship exists in a vacuum. The people around us—friends, family, sometimes even coworkers—often have strong opinions about our romantic lives. Sometimes their voices bring comfort and clarity; other times, they add pressure, judgment, or confusion.

When resentment is already simmering, external voices can amplify it or make you question yourself. Maybe your friends say, "You deserve better," or family members remind you of past hurts, or everyone expects you to "just get over it." That noise can make you feel more isolated, misunderstood, or stuck.

This section helps you navigate those echoes from the outside world. You'll learn to recognize what helps and what harms, how to protect your emotional space, and how to trust your own experience above all else. Because healing resentment is about your peace first—not anyone else's agenda.

Making Sense Of It
How Outside Forces Shape Your Resentment

Resentment doesn't grow in silence. It grows in rooms full of voices. When you're already carrying unspoken hurt, the outside commentary doesn't just float past—it seeps into you, shaping how you see yourself, your partner, and the relationship itself. And here's the hard truth: those voices don't come neutral. Every friend, sibling, parent, or coworker who weighs in brings their own ghosts, their own scars, their own unfinished business. What feels like "advice" is almost always projection.

A friend who once stayed too long with the wrong person may push you to leave faster than you're ready. A parent who fears abandonment may urge you to forgive, no matter the cost. Even silence carries weight—when people avoid the subject, you may read it as judgment or lack of support. None of this is random. Human beings have always lived in communities where love and survival were intertwined. In small tribes, who you partnered with shaped food, protection, alliances. We are still wired to think of relationships as collective property. So when people chime in on your love life, they are unknowingly reenacting something ancient: the belief that your relationship belongs, at least partly, to them.

That's why outside commentary can sting so sharply. It isn't just "input"—it's a clash of worlds. Their version of love, filtered through their history, bumping up against your lived reality. They're not just questioning your choices; in your nervous system, it can feel like they're questioning your sanity. And when resentment already thins your emotional skin, even one careless phrase—"I'd never put up with that" or "You're overreacting"—lands like salt on an open wound.

Making Sense Of It
How Outside Forces Shape Your Resentment

The danger is that you start carrying resentment in layers. Not just toward your partner, but toward the people who "don't get it." And sometimes even toward yourself—because when everyone else seems certain, and you're the one still torn, shame seeps in. You start to feel like you're failing some invisible test: the "right" response, the "brave" choice, the "enough-is-enough" moment. But here's the thing no one tells you: clarity doesn't arrive on other people's timelines. It unfolds at the pace your body and heart can bear.

And so, the question becomes: how do you separate their echoes from your own voice? Because the danger of resentment fed by outside forces is that it stops being about the original wound. Instead of asking, "What do I feel in this relationship?" you start asking, "What do they think I should feel?" That subtle shift pulls you further from your own truth.

Here's the eye-opener: most of the time, when people weigh in, they aren't talking to you at all. They're talking to the version of themselves that once felt powerless. They are speaking to their younger selves through your story. And if you take their words as gospel, you risk living out their unfinished narrative instead of your own.

That doesn't mean you should wall yourself off. Outside voices can sometimes offer clarity—reminding you of patterns you've normalized, or giving you language for what you've been swallowing. But the key difference is how it feels in your body.

Making Sense Of It
How Outside Forces Shape Your Resentment

Helpful echoes don't pressure you into action; they anchor you in self-trust. Harmful echoes leave you more confused, more ashamed, less steady.

Your task is not to stop the canyon from echoing. That's impossible. Your task is to listen differently—to notice which reverberations clarify your own sound and which twist it into something unrecognizable. Because healing resentment isn't about proving your family right, or defending your partner to your friends, or even explaining yourself until you're understood. Healing resentment is about refusing to outsource your inner compass.

The truth? No one else sleeps beside your heart at night. No one else wakes up to your silence, your longing, your dread. And no one else has to carry the consequences of staying or leaving—except you. When you realize that, the outside voices shrink back into what they truly are: echoes. Loud, sometimes persuasive, but never the origin. The origin is you.

Which people in my life comment most about my relationship, and how do their words affect me?

Reflect on whether their voices help or hurt your healing.

Which people in my life comment most about my relationship, and how do their words affect me?

How have friends or family influenced my feelings of resentment—either by validating or dismissing them?

Explore moments where external opinions shifted your inner experience.

How have friends or family influenced my feelings of resentment—either by validating or dismissing them?

Are there times I've changed how I feel or act because of others' expectations?

Notice when you might have silenced your needs to avoid conflict or judgment.

Are there times I've changed how I feel or act because of others' expectations?

What boundaries do I need to set around conversations about my relationship?

Think about limits that protect your emotional space.

What boundaries do I need to set around conversations about my relationship?

How can I communicate my needs to those close to me without feeling guilty or defensive?

Plan ways to be honest while maintaining your peace.

How can I communicate my needs to those close to me without feeling guilty or defensive?

When do I feel most alone in my resentment, despite having people around me?

Identify gaps in your emotional support system.

When do I feel most alone in my resentment, despite having people around me?

How can I remind myself that my healing is my own journey, regardless of others' opinions?

Create affirmations or rituals that reinforce self-trust.

How can I remind myself that my healing is my own journey, regardless of others' opinions?

TRACING THE TRUTH

THE PROJECTION MIRROR

Most of the time, when someone speaks into your relationship, they're not really speaking to you—they're speaking to the part of themselves still tangled in their own story. This exercise helps you spot when advice is a reflection of them more than you.

Why it helps:
This shifts the frame from "They must be right about me" to "This is their story, not mine." By naming the projection, you reclaim your ability to separate echoes from your own truth.

On the next page, there are two columns: Their Voice and Possible Projection.

Under Their Voice, write down specific advice or comments you've heard about your relationship. Example: "You need to get out now."

Under Possible Projection, ask: What experience in their life could make them say this? Write your best guess. Example: They stayed too long with someone who mistreated them.

Circle the comments that feel more about their unfinished pain than your reality.

Pause and reflect: What does my body feel when I read these words—steady, tense, or confused?

TRACING THE TRUTH

THE PROJECTION MIRROR

Their Voice	Possible Projection

TRACING THE TRUTH

THE PROJECTION MIRROR

Their Voice	Possible Projection

TRACING THE TRUTH

THE PROJECTION MIRROR

REFLECTION

TRACING THE TRUTH

THE CANYON TEST

Outside voices are like echoes in a canyon. Some bounce back clear and grounding; others come back warped and jagged. This exercise helps you tell the difference.

Why it helps:
It turns vague noise into a map. You learn which voices add clarity and which blur your inner compass, making it easier to trust your body's signals instead of everyone else's volume.

Write down three recent comments you've received about your relationship.
For each one, ask yourself: After hearing this, do I feel heavier, lighter, or confused?
Mark each with a symbol:
Grounding Echo = makes you feel steadier, clearer
Distorting Echo = leaves you anxious, ashamed, or pulled in two directions
For every Distorting Echo, write one sentence affirming: *This is an echo, not the origin of my truth.*
For every Grounding Echo, write: *This helps me reconnect with myself.*

TRACING THE TRUTH

THE CANYON TEST

TRACING THE TRUTH

THE CANYON TEST

TRACING THE TRUTH

THE CIRCLE OF CARRIERS

Imagine that every piece of advice handed to you is like someone giving you a heavy stone. If you don't sort them, you'll end up carrying a bag full of other people's rocks. This exercise helps you choose what you actually want to carry.

Why it helps:
This makes the invisible weight visible. By literally drawing the circle, you externalize the burden of other people's input and reclaim the right to decide what belongs with you—and what doesn't.

The circle on the next page if your "bag."
Around the circle, write down each person who has weighed in on your relationship. Next to their name, jot the specific message they've given you.
For each one, ask: Do I want to carry this stone? Does it make me stronger, or does it weigh me down?
If you don't want to carry it, *cross it out and write: Not mine to hold.*
Inside the circle, write only the messages you choose to keep. These are the stones you'll allow to stay in your bag.

TRACING THE TRUTH

THE CIRCLE OF CARRIERS

Making Sense Of It
The Pressure to Perform — How Expectations Shape Resentment

There's a particular kind of loneliness that comes from smiling when you're not okay. It's the performance we put on for the world — at family dinners, with friends over coffee, even in quick "how are you?" exchanges. When resentment simmers in a relationship, the outside world often doesn't want to see it. They want the polished version, the version that reassures them love works out neatly. And so you learn to wear the mask: I'm fine, we're fine, everything's fine.

But resentment doesn't vanish under a mask. It festers. Because every time you pretend, you split yourself in two — the version that looks composed and the version that aches in silence. Over time, that split can feel like betrayal against yourself. You're not just angry at your partner anymore; you're angry at the invisible script that tells you to "hold it together." That's how resentment grows roots, digging deeper, because it's not allowed to be spoken out loud.

Why does this pressure to perform exist? Part of it is cultural. We live in societies obsessed with appearances — curated feeds, holiday cards, milestone announcements. Happiness is treated as proof of worth. Struggle, on the other hand, is framed as weakness, something to be fixed quickly or hidden away. So when your relationship hits a storm, people may nudge you toward tidy narratives: "Move on already." "Don't dwell." "Stay strong." On the surface, it sounds like encouragement. Underneath, it's dismissal. The complexity of your pain doesn't fit their preferred story.

Another layer is more primal. In any close-knit group, harmony has always been prized. In ancient communities, tension between couples could ripple outward, unsettling alliances, resources, stability. That instinct hasn't disappeared.

Making Sense Of It
The Pressure to Perform — How Expectations Shape Resentment

People still crave reassurance that everything is "stable" in your corner, because instability threatens the whole. So even unconsciously, your circle may pressure you to minimize your resentment for the sake of their comfort.

The impact is corrosive. When you swallow your truth, resentment becomes not just about what your partner did or didn't do — it's about the cost of hiding it. You begin to resent the people who won't listen, the culture that demands neatness, and even yourself for playing along. That's why the performance feels so exhausting. You're not only carrying the weight of the relationship; you're carrying the weight of other people's expectations stacked on top of it.

Here's the paradox: the more you perform, the more people believe the performance. And the more they believe it, the less space you're given to be real. It becomes a self-sealing trap. But underneath the mask, your body always knows. The headaches, the tight chest, the sudden irritability — those are signs of emotions shoved underground. Resentment that's buried doesn't disappear; it mutates. It grows sharper, more tangled, harder to reach.

Breaking this cycle starts with reclaiming your right to be messy. To tell the untidy version of your story. To answer "How are you?" with something truer than "fine." Because resentment can't heal in secrecy. It softens only when it's acknowledged — first by you, then by the people safe enough to hold it.

You don't owe anyone a polished narrative. You don't owe anyone proof that you're "over it" on their timeline. Healing isn't a performance; it's a slow, uneven, deeply human process.

How do I feel when others expect me to "just get over" my resentment?

Reflect on the ways these expectations affect your emotional honesty.

How do I feel when others expect me to "just get over" my resentment?

In what ways have I hidden my true feelings to avoid judgment or disappointing others?

Explore the cost of emotional masking.

In what ways have I hidden my true feelings to avoid judgment or disappointing others?

How might releasing the need to perform for others help me in my healing?

Consider what freedom might look like without external pressure.

How might releasing the need to perform for others help me in my healing?

What would it mean to set my own timeline for healing, regardless of what others think?

Write about owning your process and pace.

What would it mean to set my own timeline for healing, regardless of what others think?

How can I create more space for authentic expression in my relationships outside my romantic one?

Brainstorm ways to foster honest connection with friends and family.

How can I create more space for authentic expression in my relationships outside my romantic one?

What affirmations can remind me that my feelings are valid, no matter what others say?

Develop personal mantras to reinforce self-trust.

What affirmations can remind me that my feelings are valid, no matter what others say?

TRACING THE TRUTH

THE MASK DRAWER

Every time you hide resentment behind a smile, it's like putting on a mask. Over time, you end up with a whole drawer full of them — "I'm fine," "We're great," "It's nothing." This exercise helps you notice which masks you wear most often, and what it costs you to keep them on.

Why it helps:
By visualizing your "mask drawer," you see how much energy goes into performance. Naming the costs exposes the quiet betrayal of hiding, and choosing one mask to retire gives you a concrete first step toward reclaiming honesty and softening resentment.

The rectangles on the next page represent boxes in a drawer.
In the first box, *Mask I Wear Most Often*, write down the exact "mask lines" you tend to say (e.g., "We're just busy," "I'm over it.").
In the second box, *Who I Wear It For*, list the people or groups you perform for — friends, family, coworkers, social media.
In the third box, *What It Costs Me*, write the hidden cost of each mask. Does it leave you drained, resentful, disconnected from yourself?
Finally, draw a small space outside the drawer and title it Mask I Want to Retire First. Write down which mask you're ready to lay down, even once, in a safe space.

TRACING THE TRUTH

THE MASK DRAWER

Mask I Wear Most Often

Who I Wear It For

What It Costs Me

FOUNDATIONS OF CALM

Our bodies and minds are deeply connected—when physical needs are neglected, emotions intensify and coping becomes harder. PLEASE encourages you to take care of your body in simple, practical ways that support emotional stability: eating regularly, sleeping well, moving your body, and avoiding substances that amplify stress or mood swings. Focusing on one small, achievable upgrade at a time helps you build sustainable habits without overwhelm. These micro-choices add up, giving your nervous system a solid foundation so your emotions and decisions feel clearer and calmer.

① Pick one small upgrade today. Example: add one glass of water, go for a 10-minute walk, or set a 15-minute wind-down before bed.

② Notice the impact. Record any shifts in mood, energy, or clarity.

CHECK IN ON BASIC BODY NEEDS

- **Physical Health** — Treat illness, take medications, follow doctor's advice.
- **Nutrition** — Eat balanced meals, hydrate.
- **Sleep** — Aim for consistent rest.
- **Movement** — Gentle exercise, stretching, or walking.
- **Substances** — Limit alcohol, nicotine, or stimulants that spike mood swings.

BALANCED MIND CHECK-IN

When emotions run high, it's easy to get pulled into extremes—either reacting purely from feelings or overthinking with logic alone. Wise Mind Access helps you pause and bring both sides together: your emotional insight and your reasoned perspective. By visualizing Emotion Mind and Reasonable Mind meeting, you create space for clarity, calm, and grounded decision-making. Writing down the first calm thought that arises captures the guidance of your "middle path," helping you respond intentionally rather than reacting impulsively.

Pause and breathe. Close your eyes and settle your body.
Visualize Emotional Mind and Reasonable Mind. See each as a part of you with its own voice.
Bring them together. Imagine them stepping closer, listening, and blending perspectives.
Ask: "What does my Wise Mind know?" Let the first calm, clear sentence emerge naturally.
Example: "I can honor my feelings while setting a boundary calmly."
Write it down. Keep it as a reference for action or reflection.

Emotional Mind　　　　　　　　　　　　　　　**Reasonable Mind**

Wise Mind

SECTION TEN

Building Your Peace — Practical Steps to Move Forward

Healing resentment isn't a one-time event — it's a process. Some days you'll feel lighter, others heavier, and that's okay. This section is about equipping you with practical tools and habits that help you build a steady foundation of peace and resilience. It's not about perfection or "fixing" the relationship overnight. It's about learning how to care for yourself, respond with intention, and create boundaries that protect your wellbeing.

You've done the hard work of understanding your resentment, setting limits, and navigating external pressures. Now, it's time to focus on daily practices that help you stay grounded when resentment tries to creep back in. These tools are about reclaiming your calm, your clarity, and your confidence — so resentment no longer steals your energy or your joy.

Making Sense Of It
Escaping The Trap

Resentment has a way of convincing you that peace only comes after the other person changes. You wait for them to apologize, to understand, to finally treat you the way you've been asking for all along. But peace built on someone else's actions is fragile. It rises and falls with their moods, their choices, their willingness. And that means your sense of safety is always in someone else's hands.

Real peace — the kind that lasts — comes from building daily practices that anchor you back into yourself. It's less about dramatic breakthroughs and more about quiet, steady habits that say, I am responsible for my own calm. When you can return to that place, resentment loses its power to hijack your days. You stop being a hostage to someone else's behavior and start cultivating an inner environment where clarity and strength can grow.

Think of resentment as a leak in your house. If left alone, it spreads quietly, warping the wood, seeping into the walls. You can scream at the rain to stop, or you can patch the roof and protect what's inside. The weather might still be unpredictable, but your home stays intact. In the same way, your peace doesn't depend on eliminating every trigger or silencing every conflict. It depends on your ability to reinforce your foundation, again and again, until it feels solid under your feet.

Anthropologically, humans have always needed practices to regulate the storms of life. Rituals, breathing patterns, communal circles — all ways of calming the body and restoring a sense of order in a chaotic world.

Making Sense Of It
Escaping The Trap

In modern life, those rituals have been stripped down, leaving us alone with stress that has nowhere to go. Building your peace means reclaiming that lineage — creating intentional practices that help your body exhale, your mind focus, and your emotions soften. The good news is that peace doesn't have to arrive all at once. It can be built like layers of sediment, slowly, consistently, until a strong ground forms beneath you. Some days it might look like journaling instead of spiraling. Other days, it's choosing silence over an argument, or taking a walk instead of replaying the same fight in your head. None of these choices erase the complexity of your relationship. But together, they create something more important: a sense that you are no longer at the mercy of resentment.

There's also power in boundaries. When you commit to daily practices, you are quietly telling yourself and others, My peace matters more than performance, more than winning an argument, more than proving a point. Boundaries are not walls that lock you away from connection — they're guardrails that keep you from veering off into old patterns. And every time you honor them, you reinforce the message: I choose to protect my calm.

Over time, these practices shift something deeper. They remind you that resentment doesn't define the entire relationship, nor does it define you. It may flare, but it doesn't have to consume. By tending to your inner world, you loosen resentment's grip on your outer world. What was once a constant hum of irritation begins to fade into background noise — not because the relationship is perfect, but because you've built something sturdier inside yourself.

What daily habits currently support my emotional wellbeing?

Identify routines or practices that help you stay grounded.

What daily habits currently support my emotional wellbeing?

Where could I add small moments of self-care or mindfulness into my day?

Think about practical ways to nurture yourself regularly.

Where could I add small moments of self-care or mindfulness into my day?

How do I notice resentment creeping in, and what helps me interrupt it?

Reflect on your warning signs and coping strategies.

How do I notice resentment creeping in, and what helps me interrupt it?

What boundaries have I set that have helped protect my peace?

Celebrate the limits you've established.

What boundaries have I set that have helped protect my peace?

How do I respond differently now compared to when resentment was controlling me?

Acknowledge your growth and shifts in behavior.

How do I respond differently now compared to when resentment was controlling me?

What challenges do I anticipate in maintaining these habits?

Prepare for obstacles and how you'll handle them.

What challenges do I anticipate in maintaining these habits?

Who can I lean on for support when I feel stuck?

Consider your support network and ways to reach out.

Who can I lean on for support when I feel stuck?

What does thriving look like for me, beyond just surviving resentment?

Visualize your healthiest emotional future.

What does thriving look like for me, beyond just surviving resentment?

TRACING THE TRUTH

THE ANCHOR LIST

When resentment flares, it can pull you into spirals of rumination or reactivity. An anchor list acts as a pre-written reminder of the small, grounding actions that bring you back to yourself.

Why it helps:
Resentment thrives on impulsive reactions. By creating an anchor list ahead of time, you give yourself a ready-made lifeline — a way to return to calm before the resentment takes over.

Write down 5–7 specific actions that calm or steady you. (*Examples: step outside for fresh air, write a 3-sentence journal entry, place one hand on my chest and breathe, text a trusted friend.*)
Keep the list somewhere visible — on your phone notes, a sticky note on your desk, or tucked in your wallet.
The next time resentment spikes, pause and choose one item from the list before reacting.
Check in after: Did this anchor me? Do I need to try a different one?

TRACING THE TRUTH

THE ANCHOR LIST

TRACING THE TRUTH

THE ENERGY BANK

Think of your energy like a bank account. Every time you ruminate, argue, or replay a fight in your head, you make a withdrawal. Every time you rest, create, or set a boundary, you make a deposit. This exercise helps you track where your energy is actually going.

Why it helps:
Resentment often feels vague, but energy doesn't lie. Seeing it mapped like a bank account makes the invisible toll visible — and gives you permission to protect your deposits and cut back on unnecessary withdrawals.

Use the two columns on the next page: *Withdrawals and Deposits.*
Under Withdrawals, list ways resentment drains you daily (e.g., overthinking, scrolling their social media, rehearsing comebacks).
Under Deposits, list small practices that restore you (e.g., listening to music, walking, reading, journaling).
At the end of each day for one week, add one real example in each column.
At week's end, review the "balance." Ask yourself: Where am I giving away too much? Where can I add more deposits?

TRACING THE TRUTH

THE ENERGY BANK

Withdrawals	Deposits

TRACING THE TRUTH

THE ENERGY BANK

Withdrawals	Deposits

TRACING THE TRUTH

THE PAUSE-AND-PIVOT PRACTICE

Resentment often hijacks the moment — snapping, shutting down, or replaying arguments before you even realize it. This simple "pause-and-pivot" helps you interrupt that cycle and reclaim choice.

Why it helps:
This practice rewires the reflex to "react now." The pause interrupts resentment's automatic grip, and the pivot creates a moment of freedom — reminding you that you always have a choice in how to respond.

When you feel resentment rise (tight chest, racing thoughts, urge to lash out), silently say the word *Pause*.
Take three slow breaths, feeling your feet press into the floor.
Ask yourself one pivoting question: Do I want to fuel this resentment, or redirect my energy toward peace?
If you choose peace, take one small pivot action — step outside, sip water, write one sentence in a notebook, or excuse yourself from the room.
Return only when you feel steadier.

COOL & RESET

Our nervous system reacts to temperature in ways that can quickly shift arousal. Cool sensations on the face or neck signal the body that danger is passing, helping to calm adrenaline and stress. Spending just a minute noticing the change gives your mind a break from racing thoughts and brings your body into a calmer state — a small but powerful way to regain presence and control.

Find a safe source of cool — a cold pack, splash of water, or even holding something cool in your hands.

Bring it gently to your face or neck. Focus on the sensation for about 60 seconds.

Notice the temperature, the pressure, the way your skin responds, and let your breathing follow the rhythm of the sensation.

GROUNDING ROOTS

When tension, anxiety, or overwhelm hits, our nervous system often leaves us feeling scattered or unanchored. This simple visualization reconnects your mind with your body and the ground beneath you. Imagining roots growing from your feet into the earth gives a sense of stability and support, while the act of exhaling and sending tension down those roots encourages the body to release held stress. Even a few moments can make your body feel heavier in a good way, steadier, and calmer.

1. Stand or sit with feet flat on the floor.

2. Take a slow breath and imagine roots growing from the soles of your feet deep into the earth.

3. On each exhale, picture tension, tightness, or overwhelm traveling down those roots into the ground.

4. Repeat for 1-3 minutes, noticing the sense of weight and calm building in your body.

SECTION ELEVEN

Who You Choose to Be Next

You've done the work of facing resentment — not just as an emotion, but as a signal, a story, and a survival strategy. You've looked at where it comes from, how it shows up, and what it costs. And maybe for the first time, you've also given yourself permission to want peace — not just in your relationship, but in your own body and mind.

This isn't the end of the work, but it is a new beginning. Now you get to choose: Who do I want to be, even if nothing around me changes? What kind of love do I want to offer — to myself first, and maybe to my partner, if it still feels right?

Resentment isn't your identity. It was a messenger. And now that you've heard it, you don't have to carry it forever. You get to walk lighter. You get to build differently. You get to be the version of you who lives with emotional integrity and softness at the same time.

Making Sense Of It
Identity After Resentment

When resentment has lived in you for a long time, it can begin to feel like part of your personality. You get used to scanning for slights, replaying conversations, or carrying invisible walls. It becomes the air you breathe — not because you're bitter by nature, but because resentment served as armor. It shielded you from deeper wounds: being dismissed, neglected, or hurt again.

But here's the shift that most people never realize: resentment was never you. It was a posture, a survival stance, a way your nervous system said, "If I hold this wall, I won't be crushed." Once you see it as a strategy rather than an identity, you unlock freedom.

The real work now is choosing who you want to be without that armor. That doesn't mean becoming naïve, boundary-less, or endlessly forgiving. It means reclaiming the qualities resentment muted — your softness, your joy, your curiosity, your ability to love without constantly bracing.

Think of it like a muscle that atrophied while you were surviving. Resentment kept you alive, but it also narrowed you. Now you get to strengthen something new: an identity rooted in integrity, calm strength, and deliberate choice.

This is the turning point: you no longer have to be defined by what was done to you, or how long you carried it. You get to decide what kind of person you are in love, in conflict, and in the quiet moments with yourself.

Who am I now that I've worked through this resentment?

Reflect on what feels different in how you think, feel, or respond.

Who am I now that I've worked through this resentment?

What values do I want to live by — even in hard moments?

Let this guide your next choices in love, communication, and boundaries.

What values do I want to live by — even in hard moments?

How can I tell when I'm acting from integrity instead of reactivity?

Describe the difference in your body, your tone, your thoughts.

How can I tell when I'm acting from integrity instead of reactivity?

What version of myself do I want to embody in future relationship challenges?

Visualize and name the traits you admire in yourself.

What version of myself do I want to embody in future relationship challenges?

How can I honor the pain that brought me here — without staying stuck in it?

Make space for the grief without letting it define you.

How can I honor the pain that brought me here — without staying stuck in it?

What does peace feel like in my body? When have I felt that before?

Return to it. Get familiar with it. Let it be your compass.

What does peace feel like in my body? When have I felt that before?

Who am I when I'm not stuck in resentment?

Go beyond the hurt. What's underneath?

Who am I when I'm not stuck in resentment?

What kind of love am I worthy of — from myself and from others?

You get to decide that now, not your past.

What kind of love am I worthy of — from myself and from others?

TRACING THE TRUTH

THE TWO SELVES LETTER

When co-parenting with someone abusive, it's easy to get pulled into overthinking. Every text or action can feel like proof of a bigger agenda. This exercise helps you separate what actually happened from the story your mind builds around it — giving you more clarity and less emotional exhaustion.

Why it helps:
This exercise separates who you were for survival from who you can be for peace. It makes the future self more tangible, while honoring the one who kept you safe.

Write two the letters.
The first is as the version of you who has carried resentment — what they fear, how they protects themselves, what they refuse to tolerate.
Then, write as the version of you who has released resentment — what you value, how you love, how you respond to conflict.
Place the two letters side by side. Notice the difference in posture, tone, and possibility.
Circle 3 qualities from the second self that you're ready to grow into right now.

TRACING THE TRUTH

THE TWO SELVES LETTER

TRACING THE TRUTH

THE TWO SELVES LETTER

TRACING THE TRUTH

THE TWO SELVES LETTER

TRACING THE TRUTH

THE TWO SELVES LETTER

TRACING THE TRUTH

THE TWO SELVES LETTER

TRACING THE TRUTH

THE TWO SELVES LETTER

PROTECTIVE BUBBLE

When emotions run high or interactions feel draining, it's easy for your energy to get scattered. Imagining a soft, light bubble around you helps create a sense of personal space and safety. Using your breath to strengthen the bubble on the inhale and filter in only what feels nourishing on the exhale trains your nervous system to notice boundaries, giving you a calm, centered feeling even in challenging situations.

Sit or stand comfortably, spine tall.

Visualize a soft bubble surrounding your body, glowing lightly.

Inhale and imagine the bubble strengthening, expanding slightly.

Exhale and let in only what nourishes — warmth, safety, or calm.

Continue for 1–3 minutes, noticing a sense of energetic protection and centeredness.

SOFT EYES RESET

When we're anxious or hypervigilant, our gaze often narrows, making the world feel tense or threatening. Softening your eyes and expanding your peripheral vision sends a signal to your nervous system that it's safe to relax. This subtle shift can reduce tension in the shoulders, jaw, and chest, helping you feel steadier and more grounded, even in moments of stress.

Sit or stand comfortably with spine tall.

Focus softly ahead, allowing your peripheral vision to widen.

Notice objects to the sides without staring directly at them.

Pay attention to how your body responds — shoulders, jaw, and breath may soften naturally.

Continue for 1–2 minutes, gently returning your focus to soft vision whenever it narrows.

STONEWELL HEALING PRESS

ASSESSMENT

HOW FAR I'VE COME

You've done the work — now let's see where you're at. Take a moment to rate these statements again with honesty and self-compassion. Notice what's shifted, what still feels raw, and what that means for your next steps.

1-10

1. I can notice early signs of resentment in my thoughts, body, or emotions before it escalates.

2. I feel capable of experiencing my emotions without letting others' actions, opinions, or expectations dictate how I feel.

3. I confidently identify and enforce personal boundaries that protect my emotional and mental wellbeing.

4. I can access a sense of calm and clarity even when tension, conflict, or judgment arises in my relationships.

5. I am able to respond to difficult situations with intention rather than acting from impulsive anger, frustration, or old patterns.

6. I trust my own insight and judgment about my relationship, even when others offer conflicting advice or opinions.

7. I can treat myself with kindness and understanding in moments when I feel stuck, resentful, or overwhelmed.

8. I feel clear and intentional about the kind of love, connection, and presence I want to offer to myself and others, independent of past hurts.

Mindset & Identity Shift Reflection

Healing changes the way you see yourself. You might notice you're less reactive in certain moments, more confident speaking up, or simply softer with yourself. This page is about spotting those shifts — the ones that show you're not the same person who started this journey.

In what ways do I see myself differently than when I started?

What beliefs about myself or others are shifting?

How has my sense of hope, strength, or trust evolved?

MOVING FORWARD

ACTION PLAN

This is your personalized roadmap for continuing growth beyond this workbook. Use this space to clarify which skills you'll keep practicing, how you'll notice early warning signs, and what concrete steps you'll take to support yourself. Remember, transformation happens one intentional step at a time.

Skills I will keep practicing regularly

Early warning signs or triggers I'll watch for:

When I notice these signs, here's what I will do:

MOVING FORWARD

ACTION PLAN

This is your personalized roadmap for continuing growth beyond this workbook. Use this space to clarify which skills you'll keep practicing, how you'll notice early warning signs, and what concrete steps you'll take to support yourself. Remember, transformation happens one intentional step at a time.

Ways I can check in with myself to monitor progress (daily, weekly, monthly):

People or supports I will reach out to if I need encouragement or accountability:

One commitment I'm making to myself right now:

RESOURCE LIST

The resources listed here are shared for informational purposes only. While they provide valuable support and tools for mental health, I am not endorsing or guaranteeing the quality, effectiveness, or availability of their services. It's important to explore these options and verify the details directly on their websites to ensure they align with your personal needs.

National Alliance on Mental Illness

www.nami.org

Offers free mental health education, peer support, and a 24/7 helpline.

Insight Timer

www.insighttimer.com

A free meditation app with thousands of guided meditations, music, and talks on mental well-being

Parenting for Mental Health

www.parentingformentalhealth.com

Offers resources, training, and advice on how parents can support their child's mental health, including guides and printable resources

Crisis Text Line

www.crisistextline.org

Offers free, 24/7 text-based support for mental health crises

7 Cups

www.7cups.com

Offers free, anonymous online chat with trained volunteers, as well as paid therapy with licensed professionals.

Holding on to resentment can feel like holding on to yourself — to what's right, to what hurt, to what was never repaired. Letting that go can feel like a betrayal, like giving up the only proof that it mattered. But resentment isn't proof. It's a cage. And the work you've done here — it's you reaching for the key. Letting go doesn't mean it was okay. It doesn't mean you're naive, or that you've forgotten what happened. It just means you're making space. Space for your nervous system to breathe. Space for your energy to return to you. Space for peace that isn't dependent on someone else finally understanding. Even if things stay messy. Even if they never apologize. You still get to choose a life that isn't shaped by bitterness. You get to be someone who's lived through hard things and still chose clarity over chaos. That kind of peace isn't passive — it's power. And you did something big here. Maybe no one will see it but you, but that's enough. You're who matters most now. Come back to yourself, again and again. You're allowed to have ease. You're allowed to feel safe. And if resentment tries to pull you back, remember: you know how to set yourself free.

From one human heart to another: I know how heavy it is to love and hurt at the same time — and I want you to know, I built this for the part of you that still hopes for peace. Some things won't ever feel fair — but you still deserve a life that feels free.

M. Tourangeau
Stonewell Healing Press

www.ingramcontent.com/pod-product-compliance
Lightning Source LLC
Chambersburg PA
CBHW080834230426
43665CB00021B/2835